THE FIGHT OF EVERY BELIEVER

Conquering the Thought Attacks That War Against Your Mind

by Terry Law

Harrison House
Tulsa, Oklahoma

Author emphasis in Scripture quotations in italic.

10 09 08 07 06   10 9 8 7 6 5 4 3 2

The Fight of Every Believer:
Conquering the Thought Attacks That War Against Your Mind
ISBN-13: 978-1-57794-580-2
ISBN-10: 1-57794-580-8
Copyright © 2006 by Terry Law
Terry Law Ministries
P.O. Box 92
Tulsa, OK 74101

Published by Harrison House, Inc.
P.O. Box 35035
Tulsa, Oklahoma 74153

Contents

Introduction v

Chapter 1   Playing Mind Games 1

Chapter 2   Stop, Turn, and Go in a New Direction................19

Chapter 3   "What Is It About This Book?"—The Word 35

Chapter 4   Tap Into Divine Power, Part 1—
The Name of Jesus..61

Chapter 5   Tap Into Divine Power, Part 2—
The Name of Jesus..77

Chapter 6   No Longer Guilty, Part 1—
The Blood of Jesus 87

Chapter 7   No Longer Guilty, Part 2—
The Blood of Jesus 101

Chapter 8   Your Mouth Is the Launching Pad....................113

Chapter 9   Hope: The Mind's Defense, Part 1 135

Chapter 10   Hope: The Mind's Defense, Part 2 151

Conclusion 161

Scriptures 163

Introduction

As long as we live on this earth there will be battles. Probably the most prominent one these days is the physical battle we're involved in against terrorism. We hear so much about it that it has made our nation feel more vulnerable and anxious than ever before.

Terrorism was something that always took place somewhere else, in someone else's country, not ours. But after years of threats against the United States, terrorists finally brought their fight to our soil, our homeland. Since September 11, 2001, our innocence has been replaced with a heightened sense of alertness and helplessness, prompted by a poorly defined danger that could strike at any time, in any form, anywhere.

As a whole, people are living in a chronic state of fear, especially about the future. They are afraid of possible terrorist attacks, afraid of the conflict in the Middle East, and afraid of what's happening around the world. There is a real spirit of anxiety at work, especially in our land. You can easily catch that spirit just by watching the evening news.

Such is the paradox of fear—the mother of all negative emotions. It is a response fundamental to survival, yet it shackles us, diminishes our lives, and kills us. But none of this has caught God by surprise, and He has provided what we need not only to cope, but also to overcome the strategies of the real enemy, Satan.

Second Corinthians 10:3-5 tells us that our war is not against flesh and blood, but against spiritual strongholds.[1] We must fight them with spiritual weapons. Where is our battlefield? Fear and wrong thoughts are front and center in this spiritual war because our thoughts affect our life. That's why the enemy attacks us in the battlefield of the mind.

So what have you got to fight with? I believe that God has put in your hands the most powerful weaponry in the universe. In these pages I'm going to share with you what the Lord has revealed to me from His Word concerning spiritual warfare so you will know your spiritual weapons and be able to use them to defeat the enemy.

Know Your Weapons

Back in the early days of my ministry, I didn't realize the power of the spiritual weapons God has provided to tear down spiritual strongholds established by the enemy. I knew that the Bible talked about spiritual warfare and our weapons; I had known all those things since I was quite young. But I did not fully understand the principles of spiritual warfare or the specific function of the weapons at my disposal.

Now, because of what the Lord has revealed to me through personal experiences and a more enlightened understanding of God's Word, I am much better equipped to walk in victorious Christian living and ministry. And I'm better able to fulfill my job as an evangelist, which is to teach the body of Christ how to fight the thought systems of the enemy.

That is why you need to read this book.

I am constantly amazed when I ask believers, "If you were placed in a situation where you had to face Satan's thoughts, what are your spiritual weapons?" Most of them stare at me with a blank look on their face and say, "I don't know."

If you are going to be successful in your walk with God, you must learn your enemy and know your weapons. When a soldier enters the military, one of the first things he receives is a weapon. He must learn to take it apart and then put it back together again. He becomes so proficient that he can do it in the dark because he knows that his weapon can save his life or his buddy's life.

The spiritual weapons with which God has equipped believers are no ordinary weapons. They are life-saving. According to 2 Corinthians 10:4 they are *mighty* weapons, so mighty that with them we are able to tear down any strongholds that have been established by Satan.

When you get a revelation of this truth, it will change your life. No longer will the enemy be able to run roughshod over you with sickness, poverty, depression, strife, anger, fear, or any other thing that he would use in his attempt to destroy you. You have weapons that are mighty enough to overcome anything the devil brings your way.

Guard Your Thoughts

The real problem, then, is the enemy's thought attack that believers encounter every day of their lives. All spiritual weapons have to deal with thoughts, so we're going to keep coming back to the whole idea of thoughts and direct our weapons toward dealing with them.

There is a great misunderstanding in the body of Christ about our weapons. It can hinder you from living an overcoming life. Weapons will do very little good if you're not guarding your thoughts. The enemy can drop thoughts into our minds very easily, so one thing we're going to explore is using hope to protect the way we think. No thought system has more power to protect the mind than hope.

Basically, to have hope is to expect good and not bad. If you're in a hopeless state right now, if you've somehow lost hope, I encourage you to read on because I believe that this book will help bring hope back into your life.

You are not going to overcome the enemy if you do not know how to control your thoughts and use these weapons. You can go to church until the cows come home, but you will never walk in victory. But once you do learn and have tasted victory, you will be changed. You will begin to expect success instead of defeat.

God did not create you to lose; He created you to win. And He's given you the weapons by which you can obtain that victory. I believe that as you learn how to use your spiritual weapons, you will move into a power with God that you've never known before—power to tear down the enemy's strongholds in your life. That's power for maximum effect!

CHAPTER 1

Playing Mind Games

Though we walk in the flesh, we do not war according to the flesh.

For the weapons of our warfare are not carnal but mighty in God for pulling down strongholds.

casting down arguments and every high thing that exalts itself against the knowledge of God, bringing every thought into captivity to the obedience of Christ.

2 Corinthians 10:3-5

We are at war—not only against terrorism, but in our lives personally. In this passage, the apostle Paul addresses the war in which all believers fight. He is talking to each one of us because we live in flesh on this earth. This passage of Scripture will apply to us as long as we are here. But notice it says, "we do not war according to the flesh." In other words, our war is not a war that we see with our physical eye. We are warring in another dimension—the realm of the spirit.

The weapons God has given us to fight this war are not carnal or earthly but spiritual; they are "mighty through God for pulling down strongholds." The two primary words in that verse are *weapons* and *strongholds,* but we're going to look at verse four first.

What are strongholds? I describe them as evil spiritual beings that work directly with the devil. They study us and know us better than we know ourselves. They operate through the medium of thought. They are at war with us, and we are at war with them. Either they are going to win, or we are going to win. We've got to make up our minds that we will win. Why? Because we have mighty weapons, as Paul says, to pull them down.

We spend a lot of time and energy trying to cope with life. We learned ways to defend ourselves that were not necessarily healthy. We developed defense mechanisms that involved our thought life. Some people continually make excuses for poor behavior. Others are continually withdrawn because they are afraid of rejection. And then there are the "pass the buck" artists who blame others. These defense mechanisms are "strongholds" in our thought life.

A stronghold is like a mindset. We are held in bondage by a certain way of thinking. We may think we are ugly, for example. The enemy suggests that you play a thought over and over in your head a thousand times. *I am ugly.* After years of thinking this, you have a stronghold. It's not going to go away overnight. This is where you use your weapons. If you are dealing with habitual confusion or are plagued by constant doubt or anxiety and fear—you are dealing with a stronghold.

Before we were born again, we constantly programmed these fleshly thought patterns into our minds. After our new birth experience, these patterns were not automatically erased. If we learned them over time, then we must unlearn them over time by using our weapons. This book is about reprogramming our minds to think like Jesus. Let me caution you again, however; it's going to take some time. You must decide to exercise your spiritual weapons persistently.

What does pulling down strongholds mean?

In Ephesians 6:12 Paul tells us, "We do not wrestle against flesh and blood." That means that your problem is not with people. Although people may be causing problems for you, they are not the real problem. The problem is the spirits that operate behind the people, and that's what we've got to learn to deal with. We've got to learn how to pull those strongholds down.

How do strongholds operate? They come against us in our thoughts. The strongholds we are to pull down in our lives are the thought patterns that the enemy has built into our minds or is trying to build in our minds. Day and night he bombards us with negative thoughts and lies designed to destroy our spiritual life.

Area of Conflict

Our thought life can be tremendously affected when someone says something negative about us. Or the enemy, Satan, may put a thought in our mind that we take hold of. Have you ever thought, *I'm no good, I continue to fail all the time,* or *I don't know if I can ever be a really good Christian?* These are thoughts that are planted by the enemy. There are entire religions and political ideologies that are based on thought systems—Islam and Communism, for example.

Satan is an expert in thought systems. He uses them to contradict the authenticity of Scripture. But, thank God, we're not left at the mercy of the enemy. In 2 Corinthians 10:4, Paul talks about pulling down strongholds, and in verse 5 he tells us the way to deal with them. The *King James Version* says it like this:

Casting down imaginations, and every high thing that exalteth itself against the knowledge of God, and bringing into captivity every thought to the obedience of Christ.

The most common way the spiritual world interacts with the physical world is through the human thought process. If God wants to do something in the world, He speaks to the spirits of His children. If the devil wants to do something in the world, he speaks through the imaginations and thoughts of people. This is important to recognize because our thoughts have great potential power. Proverbs 23:7 KJV puts it this way: "As he [a man] thinketh in his heart, so is he."

If you want to find out how Satan is operating in your life, don't look for him with split hooves way out in the universe somewhere. Check what's going on between your own two ears, because that is the area of conflict. Thoughts are how he attacks your life. This is how he has access to you.

The Good News of the gospel is that as believers we have victory over the devil because Christ defeated him at Calvary. When we become born again, we are in Christ. He stripped Satan of his power, so the only way Satan can defeat us is if we buy into his deception and lies. That means that we can defeat him by bringing every thought and imagination into captivity to the obedience of Christ.

The Message Bible says it this way: "We use our powerful God-tools [our weapons] for smashing warped philosophies, tearing down barriers erected against the truth of God, fitting every loose thought and emotion and impulse into the structure of life shaped by Christ."

The Foundation of Sin

I call the devil's use of thoughts to defeat us "thought attack," or "thought systems." He revealed his *modus operandi* right from the beginning, in the Garden of Eden. He is still doing the same thing today.

*The serpent was more subtil than any beast of the field which the Lord God had made. And he said unto the woman, Yea, **hath God said,** Ye shall not eat of every tree of the garden?*

...Ye shall not surely die:

For God doth know that in the day ye eat thereof, then your eyes shall be opened, and ye shall be as gods, knowing good and evil.

Genesis 3:1,4,5 KJV

Satan spoke a mere three words to Eve that became the foundation of sin in the entire human race: "Hath God said?" Sin began with a thought that the devil sowed in the heart of Eve. He tempted her to doubt what God had said, and sin was born when she began to believe Satan's words of doubt. Along with her husband, Adam, she ate the forbidden fruit.

In fact, doubting the Word of God is always at the root of sin. When you least expect it, the enemy will introduce a thought that is contrary to God's Word. It will come in a flash of time, in a moment when you're not prepared, and will cause you to question what you believe. If these thoughts are not cast down and brought into captivity to the obedience of Christ—which means you realign your thinking with Scripture—they can become strongholds.

Strongholds Over Cities

Looking into a city's early history often reveals spiritual forces that still operate in that city today. A biblical example of this can be found in Daniel 10:20. This verse refers to "the prince of Persia," an evil spiritual stronghold representing that hostile world power,[1] who attempted to hinder the answer to Daniel's prayer. Let me give you a present-day example from personal experience.

Many years ago I was traveling in Sweden with *Living Sound,* my music group, and we were evangelizing in the city of Stockholm. We were a large group, and there weren't enough homes for us to stay in, so our sponsors provided lodging downtown in the YMCA. What I didn't know was that this area of the city was filled with prostitution.

I went to bed that first night in a normal fashion and slept peacefully for a while. At about three o'clock in the morning I suddenly woke up with some of the most grotesque, sexually perverse thoughts that had ever come into my mind. They were so foreign to any thought patterns I was used to that I was shocked.

I believe that people are particularly prone to negative thoughts in that twilight zone time when we're half awake and half asleep, just as we are when we first drift off to sleep. I think that this "twilight zone" area is probably when the enemy launches thought attacks against us more than any other time.

As I was slowly waking up and coming to consciousness, I became aware that I was thinking these lustful, horrible thoughts. It felt as if a clamp were on my brain and a vice were pushing on my head, and I remember thinking, *I'm awful. I've done something terribly wrong. I'm guilty.* I had a wave of guilt for having such thoughts. So I started to pray in the Spirit while still lying on the bed.

The thought attack continued for about fifteen minutes, until I realized that I was filled with the Word of God, which meant that these thoughts were not my normal thoughts and that I could command this thing to leave me alone. I came off the bed, walked to the window, and said, "Satan is a liar; the Word of God says that I have the mind of Christ" (1 Cor. 2:16), and I commanded that evil spirit to get out of there. When I did, I felt the vice come off my head. Then for some reason I looked out the window, and what I saw made me realize what had just happened to me.

The street was full of prostitutes who were plying their trade. As I looked at that scene, I realized that certain evil spirits, like the spirit of lust that had attacked my thoughts, rule over areas in some cities.

When you come into areas where spirits like that are predominant, you open yourself up to those thought systems, which can bring you into guilt and condemnation over wrong thinking. If you don't know what to do about it—if you don't rebuke it and stand against it with the Word—you will take ownership of your thoughts. You won't realize what you're dealing with and you'll fall into the enemy's trap.

It's not just thoughts of lust, either. It can be thoughts of anger, violence, or anything that the enemy is counting on to bring you down. It's out there. It's a reality that we need to learn to deal with because certain thought systems rule over certain cities and some of the people within them.

Pulling Down Strongholds

I was driving down the road several years ago listening to a tape from a prophetic conference. The person preaching began to talk about the thought systems that are dominant over some cities. One of the spirits and cities he named was a spirit of violence in Chicago, which is true historically. Most people are certainly familiar with the infamous gangster Al Capone and the reign of violence that he established.

The conference speaker went on to say that there was a spirit of sexual perversion in San Francisco, a spirit of the occult in New Orleans, a spirit of religious confusion in Boston, and then he said something that stunned me. He said there is a spirit of political confusion in Miami. I heard these words just after the contested election results involving George Bush and Al Gore in 2000. What was astounding was that the tape I was listening to had been recorded in 1987. The whole world had just been witness to a manifestation of the spirit of political confusion in Miami-Dade County, Florida.

What happened in the early days of a city is basic to the spiritual life of that city. When you examine it, you'll find that those strongholds are able to operate and that they have been given freedom to operate within a certain area. If allowed to, they will exercise certain kinds of powers and thought systems against the minds of unsuspecting people who live there or travel there.

I'll never forget when I was ministering in a city in western Canada. I was introduced to a little woman who was being controlled by evil spirits that had attacked her mind. Her Christian friends brought her to the meeting from a mental institution. She had been in a straightjacket and had not spoken a word in over a year. The spirits that were controlling her made her physically sick in the parking lot, so they brought her through a side door into a Sunday school room so she could hear the Word of the Lord. I didn't know she was there.

I began to preach. There was a tremendous anointing in the service that night. Afterward, the pastor brought me to the Sunday school room and asked if I could help the woman. In the natural my heart sank as I looked at her. Her eyes were half shut, and she looked like a zombie. But a compassion rose up inside me, and I knew it was an anointing of the Holy Spirit.

I said to the little woman, "I don't know if you can understand me or not, but I'm going to suggest one thing. Don't hang on to those things that are holding you. If you want to be delivered and set free of them, then you let them go when I command them to leave you, and you speak to them as I do."

I sensed just a glimmer of recognition on her face, and then I began to command those spirits in Jesus' name. The first spirit named itself. When I came to the sixth spirit, I asked, "What's your name?"

That spirit said, "My name is mind control."

I said, "Mind control, in Jesus' name, come out." And when I said that, I felt something lift off her.

She looked at me and began to smile. She said, "Oh, I can remember."

When we were done, the tears were rolling down her cheeks. She left that room with her hands in the air, singing and praying in the Holy Spirit. She was saved, healed, and filled with the Holy Spirit that night.

We are in a war with thoughts that are directed against us by the enemy and unleashed in waves against the church. But, as we saw in this story, there is power in the mighty weapons of spiritual warfare such as the name of Jesus. God has given these weapons to us to pull down strongholds or thoughts.

Imaginations and Thoughts

I may be saying something that seems radical, but I believe that I can back it up with the Word of God. I have ministered all over the world, and I've dealt with evil spirits in many countries. One thing I've learned is that most of the demonic spirits that are mentioned in the Bible operate as imaginations and thoughts. Let's look at a few of them.

The spirit of fear: The apostle Paul told us that "God has not given us a spirit of fear" (2 Tim. 1:7), yet this is one of the most common spirits that I encounter in my ministry. Fear is a thought. Of course, there is a normal fear that is good. For instance, when an eighteen-wheeler comes down the road, it is wise for you to step out of the way. But when fear becomes an absolute compulsion, it becomes more than just normal fear, which means the enemy has become involved.

The spirit of lying: Lying first begins with a thought. Ananias and Sapphira are great examples of this spirit at work. We will take a closer look at them later on, but basically a thought caused them to lie to the apostle Peter and to God. It cost them their lives. And in 1 Kings 22:21-22, the Bible specifically identifies a lying spirit working through false prophets when they prophesied before Ahab and Jehoshaphat. Let me be careful to say that just because someone lies doesn't mean that they are controlled by an evil spirit. Any person can lie and know that they are lying.

The spirit of anger: Anger begins as a thought. Most likely, this is the evil spirit that troubled King Saul and motivated him to throw a javelin at David. (1 Sam. 18:8,10,11.) The prophet Isaiah told us a good way to avoid anger, "You [God] will keep him in perfect peace, whose mind is stayed on You" (Isa. 26:3).

The spirit of heaviness: Heaviness, or what we commonly call depression, begins as a thought. Isaiah 61:3 KJV instructs us how to pull down this stronghold: "To appoint unto them that mourn in Zion, to give unto them beauty for ashes, the oil of joy for mourning, the garment of praise for the spirit of heaviness."

Satan has always used these evil thoughts to beguile the human race. You experience them in your life every day. They try to drag you down. They point an accusing finger at you. They endeavor to rob you of the victory and your walk with Jesus Christ. But in this book you're going to find out how to overcome them and bring your thoughts into captivity.

When Paul tells us to bring our thoughts into captivity in 2 Corinthians 10:5, he uses an interesting Greek word for *thought*. It is the word *noema*.[2] He uses this same word in 2 Corinthians 2:11 so that no advantage would be taken of us by Satan: "For we are not ignorant of his devices," or *noema*.[3] Devices or schemes come from the same root word in the Greek language. In 2 Corinthians 4:3-4 he writes, "But even if our gospel is veiled, it is veiled to those who are perishing, whose minds the god of this age has blinded, who do not believe, lest the light of the gospel of the glory of Christ, who is the image of God, should shine on them." And again in 2 Corinthians 11:3, "But I fear, lest somehow, as the serpent deceived Eve by his craftiness, so your minds [noema][4] may be corrupted from the simplicity that is in Christ." Satan uses his thought devices to close minds to the gospel. He deceives people by corrupting their minds or thoughts by his craftiness.

Paul calls on us to renew our minds in Romans 12:1-2. Fleshly thoughts must be replaced. In Philippians 4:6-7, Paul says that we are not to be anxious about anything. Rather, in everything by prayer, we turn to God, "and the peace of God, which surpasses all under-standing, will guard your hearts and minds [noema] through Christ

Jesus. Then in Philippians 4:8 he counsels us to think thoughts that are true, noble, just, pure, lovely, and of good report.

Sickness and Thoughts

One day I asked a reputed surgeon and medical executive who was the director of a major hospital in the Midwest, "In dealing with all the surgeries and the diseases that you do, how much of what you treat is thought-based?"

His answer surprised me. "There's no question. At least two-thirds, and probably more, of disease has its foundation in thoughts. It is called psychosomatic illness." That is precisely what the Bible says, as we saw in Proverbs 23:7: "For as he [a man] thinketh in his heart, so is he."

Many in the medical and scientific community are acknowledging that our thoughts can affect our health. For example, they say that constant low-grade fear and adrenaline surges can damage the heart, raising the risk of cardiovascular disease. It can dampen the immune system, leaving stressed people more vulnerable to infection and possibly even cancer. People are increasingly reporting headaches, insomnia, back pain, neck pain, and disorientation; but after physical examination, doctors are unable to find a physical cause.

A science called psychoimmunology deals with this, connecting the mind's role to the immune system in helping to fight disease. And in some medical circles, healthy thinking is starting to be recognized as preventive medicine.[5]

I have seen how negative thinking can be harmful to a person's health. I knew a man who repeatedly declared to his brothers and his wife that he would never live to be forty. His wife would tell him not to say that, but he didn't listen to her. Eventually he got a very rare brain tumor and died about three months before his fortieth birthday. I believe that the power of his thoughts had a direct impact on his body.

Crucified by a Thought

Did you know that Jesus Christ was crucified by a thought? Remember, Satan has never changed his *modus operandi*. He used the same tactic against Jesus that he used against Eve in the Garden.

> *During supper* **the devil had already suggested to Judas Iscariot,** *Simon's son, that this was the night to carry out his plan to betray Jesus.*

> John 13:2 TLB

The *New King James Version* states it this way: "...the devil having already put it into the heart of Judas Iscariot, Simon's son, to betray Him." The devil put the *thought* to betray Jesus into Judas's heart, and the rest of that story is history.

Ananias and Sapphira

In the story of Ananias and Sapphira, Ananias sinned by lying about the price he had received from the sale of a piece of property. In Acts 5:3, Peter turned to Ananias and said,

> *Ananias, why has* **Satan filled your heart to lie** *to the Holy Spirit, and keep back part of the price of the land for yourself?*

...Why have you conceived this thing in your heart? You have not lied to men but to God.

Acts 5:3,4

Upon hearing Peter's words, Ananias dropped dead. Later that day, Sapphira, who didn't know what had transpired with Ananias, told the same lie to Peter, and she too dropped dead. The enemy had filled their hearts with a lie, and the lie destroyed them because they bought the thought of Satan.

Evil Thoughts Don't Make a Person Evil

Most of us, when a tempting thought comes, think, *Oh that's me. I'm bad. I can't believe I thought something like that.*

The fact that you think an evil thought does not make you evil. The devil has the ability to attack your mind with thoughts, but when those thoughts come, you do not have to receive them. They are not your thoughts. The truth is, the devil can't *make* you think something, but he can suggest it to you. It's your personal decision to allow your mind to think and meditate on it. The fact that the thought is presented to you is not sin. When you meditate on the thought and make it your own, then you buy the thought.

When the temptation to sin comes, God has given you the right to stop that thought and say, "That thought does not come from the Word of God, nor does it come out of my spirit. I do not receive it, Satan. In Jesus' name, I refuse to meditate on this thought."

On the other hand, if you feel guilty as soon as you think a sinful thought, then you've bought it bag and baggage. The devil has you right where he wants you. He has been binding Christians for many years using this fiendishly clever battle tactic.

As soon as the thought comes, we think, *Oh, no, here I go again. I am going down under the control of my thoughts. It's just as bad to think a thing as to do it, and I've already thought it, so I might as well just go ahead and do it.*

Paul instructed us to cast down those imaginations. That means that you have control over your thoughts. That old Flip Wilson line, "The devil made me do it," does not stand up in the light of the Word of God. The devil cannot make you do anything. You are responsible for the thoughts that occupy your mind. Remember—he suggested it initially.

Number One Priority

Not only does Satan use thoughts to influence people, but when God works through people, He usually begins with a thought. The difference is that a thought from God is based upon the Word. In Matthew 16:13 KJV Jesus asked His disciples, "Who do men say that I, the Son of Man, am?"

Peter replied, "You are the Christ, the Son of the living God" (v. 16).

Jesus responded to Peter's answer in verse 17:

"Blessed are you, Simon Bar-Jonah: for flesh and blood has not revealed this to you, but My Father who is in heaven."

In other words, Jesus said, "God has just given you a thought, Peter." As a result of that thought, Peter was the first disciple to declare that Jesus was the Son of God. He received approbation from the Master.

A few minutes later Jesus began to explain to the disciples that He was going to suffer many things at the hands of the chief priests and scribes, that He would be killed and then raised on the third day.

But Peter rebuked Him, saying, "Far be it from You, Lord; this shall not happen to You!" (v. 22).

Then Jesus turned to the same person to whom He had given approbation ten minutes before and said, "Get behind Me, Satan!" (v. 23).

Jesus wasn't calling Peter Satan. He was referring to Satan as being the source of the thought that had entered Peter's mind and had caused him to speak contrary to God's Word.

It's incredible that within the span of a few minutes, Peter received thoughts from God as well as thoughts from the devil. This is a classic, biblical revelation of this phenomenon. We can receive revelation and uplifting Word-based thoughts from God, but we are also vulnerable to receiving what I call "thought attacks" from the devil.

There's much more power in God's thoughts than in the devil's thoughts. But if you entertain and meditate on the devil's thoughts instead of God's thoughts, you will eventually sin. For example, if you watch soap operas on television (I call them "As The Stomach Turns" and "Die Nasty") and start thinking those thoughts and imagining adultery and lies and the twisted morals that are presented in those programs, those sins will start manifesting in your life.

In the same way, when you open your Bible and read it daily, you're setting the stage for God in your life, for God to intersect with you, for God to intervene in your life, and for His healing and blessing to come pouring over you. But that can't happen if you're not giving His thoughts (which are in His Word) number one priority over everything else you do. How important is that? Your life can be transformed by the power of just one thought from God.

You Can Overcome Strongholds

Let me summarize the whole issue of thoughts by these three simple facts: 1) We cannot choose *not* to think. 2) We cannot think two thoughts at the same time. In other words, we cannot think God's thoughts and the devil's thoughts at the same time. 3) We can choose which thoughts we want to dwell on. We can choose *what* we think about.

Let's look at the Parable of the Sower regarding thoughts.

When anyone hears the word of the kingdom, and does not understand it, then the wicked one comes, and snatches away what was sown in his heart.

Matthew 13:19

The devil can snatch the truth of God out of the heart of a person. One of the ways he does this is through the power of suggestion.

Have you ever noticed on Sunday morning when you are sitting in church, the pastor is saying something good from the Word, but you find your thoughts wandering? You don't think something evil or wicked, just something that takes your attention away from the Word.

You may be planning a business trip and are leaving on Monday morning. Or you may be planning the menu for your family for the next week. These are not evil suggestions—just random thoughts that take your mind off the Word.

Satan is more active on Sunday morning than at any other time in the week. He is trying to snatch away what God wants to sow in our hearts.

Understanding that will go a long way in helping you overcome the strongholds of the enemy. The enemy operates in the area of your thoughts, and he tries to play mind games on you physically, emotionally, spiritually—in every area of your life—because he's out to destroy you.

I'm not talking theory here, just the Word of God. Jesus told us what the enemy wants to do to us in John 10:10.

"The thief does not come except to steal, and to kill, and to destroy."

The weapons God has provided for us, identified in His Word as spiritual weapons, deal with three primary areas of thought attack: 1) temptation, 2) deception, and 3) accusation. This chapter on thought attack has presented the problem and revealed the battle every believer goes through. Now we're going to analyze Satan's attacks in these three specific areas and look at the weapons we are to use to thwart them.

Satan may be an expert at tempting, deceiving, and accusing, but we can fight him with weapons that are designed specifically by God to counter whatever the enemy throws at us.

CHAPTER 2

Stop, Turn, and Go in a New Direction

I remember traveling from Amsterdam to London in August of 1998. When I checked in at the Excelsior Hotel at Heathrow Airport, I was informed that our American President was going to address the nation concerning his sexual dalliance with one of his female White House interns. That evening there was great interest in the hotel about the program. It aired at 3 A.M. on all the primary British networks— BBCI, BBCII, ITV, and Sky News. I watched his confession of guilt to the American people.

When he was done speaking, the commentators began their customary spin. As I switched from channel to channel there was one question that most of them were asking. "Did he repent?" Some seemed to think he did; others seemed to think he did not.

What I noticed was that none of the commentators was able to define what true repentance means. I said to myself, *I am going to research this subject.* When I came home to Tulsa, I asked my secretary to find every book on repentance in our Christian bookstores. After a futile search, I was thunderstruck to find out that I could not find one book on that subject in the stores.

Repentance is the first word of the gospel. Jesus preached in Mark 1:15, "Repent, and believe in the gospel." He declared that repentance and remission of sins should be preached to all nations. (Luke 24:47.) On the day of Pentecost Peter said, "Repent, and be baptized every one of you" (Acts 2:38 KJV). Whatever has become of our teaching on this foundational doctrine of the Christian faith? (See Heb. 6:1-2.) Understanding repentance means understanding how we deal with our thoughts.

Many Christians come to God and don't really settle the issue of whether they belong to God or the devil. The one thing that often startles me about this is the fact that many don't seem to have any kind of understanding of repentance. There's conjecture but no plumbline as to what repentance is or what it does. So before we look at our spiritual weapons, I'm going to address this subject because repentance is a central part of how our thoughts are changed. It's actually a thought process that is fundamental to Christian faith.

Do you know what the Bible means when it says "repent"?

As a boy growing up in a classical Pentecostal church, I was led to believe that when people repented, they would go to the altar and cry. But crying has nothing to do with repentance and what it means.

The New Testament word for "repentance" in the Greek language is *metanoia,* and it has always had one clear meaning. From the classical Greek of the days of Plato, Aristotle, and Socrates through the Greek of the New Testament, repentance has meant "to change one's mind or to change the way one thinks." It's all about our thoughts.

Repentance Is Not Penance

You've heard the story that, crawling up the steps of a cathedral in Rome, Martin Luther tried to buy the grace of God through penance. But then came the revelation that "The just shall live by faith" (Rom. 1:17). It was tradition that taught him that penance would somehow earn the favor of God.

Penance and repentance are not the same thing. In the New Testament, *repentance* means to change your mind. The Old Testament Hebrew meaning for *repentance* is interesting and a little different from the New Testament meaning. In the Old Testament, one meaning of *repentance* is to turn, to return, or to turn back.[1] In other words, you are going one way, but then you turn or return; you go back the other way.

In essence, repentance is a 180-degree turn. It means that your actions are taking you along a pathway in one direction, but God convicts you of sin. Then you repent, and you stop going that way. You turn around and go back in the opposite direction, diametrically opposed to the direction that you had been going.

If you put together the New Testament Greek meaning with the Old Testament Hebrew, you could say that *repentance* is an inner change of mind resulting in an outward turning around to walk in a completely new direction.

An Old Testament Example

As I began to study repentance, I looked into the story of David and Bathsheba in the Old Testament. (See 2 Sam. 11.) David committed adultery with Bathsheba. To cover his sin, he had her husband, Uriah, killed while on the battlefield. To sum it up, David was an adulterer and a murderer. For a year he thought no one knew what he had done.

One day God sent Nathan the prophet to David with a story about a poor man with a special ewe lamb that his children loved. The man's next-door neighbor was a rich man. One day a traveler visited the house of the rich man, and instead of the rich man killing one of his own lambs to feed the guest, he took the poor man's precious ewe lamb.

Nathan asked David what should be done to the rich man, and David replied, "The man who has done this shall surely die!" (2 Sam. 12:5).

Then, in one of the most dramatic moments in the Old Testament, Nathan pointed his finger at King David and said, "You are the man!" (v. 7).

That was an incredible moment, but David saw his sin and truly repented, saying, "I have sinned against the Lord" (v. 13). That is what made David a man after God's own heart. He was a great sinner, but he was also a great repenter.

The Cry of True Repentance

In the *King James Version* of the Bible, there is a caption at the beginning of Psalm 51 that reads, "A psalm of David, when Nathan the prophet came unto him, after he had gone in to Bath-sheba."

Have mercy upon me, O God, according to thy lovingkindness: according unto the multitude of thy tender mercies blot out my transgressions.

Wash me thoroughly from mine iniquity, and cleanse me from my sin.

For I acknowledge my transgressions: and my sin is ever before me. Against thee, thee only, have I sinned, and done this evil in thy sight.

Create in me a clean heart, O God; and renew a right spirit within me.

Cast me not away from thy presence; and take not thy holy spirit from me.

Psalm 51:1–4,10,11 KJV

Notice that the first verse of this psalm begins, "Have mercy upon me, O God." This is the cry of a man who is repenting. Was this the cry of your heart when you came to God?

God forgave David, and the shocking truth is that He forgave David so completely that Jesus Christ was born through the bloodline of David and Bathsheba! To our natural minds, that doesn't seem right, but that is the result of what true repentance means in the kingdom of God.

The Story of Esau

Esau was another Old Testament figure who could have been in the lineage of Jesus. He was the older of twins born to Isaac and Rebekah. Genesis 25 describes Esau as being a hairy man, a hunter, and an adventurer. His twin brother, Jacob, on the other hand, was very ordinary and kept flocks near home, a mother's boy.

One day Esau had been out looking for game and came back to the campfire famished. Jacob was preparing a stew, which Esau smelled. He said to Jacob, "I've got to have some of that or I'm going to die."

Jacob, whose name means deceiver or supplanter,[2] said, "Okay, Esau, I'll give it to you. But I tell you what. I'll give you the pottage if you will sell me your birthright."

Now this may sound like only a Sunday school story, but we don't understand what the birthright meant in those days. It was a very sacred gift, the highest honor that a father could bestow upon his eldest son. It meant that the priesthood of the family would descend from the father to the eldest son and that the eldest son would become the priest to all the children.

It also meant that the grace and divine promises of God would descend primarily upon the eldest son. When someone sold his birthright, he was, in essence, selling the grace of God and the promises that were meant for him. Think of it—Esau sold his genealogical position in the lineage of Jesus Christ. His name is not even mentioned in the four Gospels. Jacob, on the other hand, is the one who is listed in both Matthew 1:2 and Luke 3:34 as a forefather of Jesus. Esau gave it all up—all for a bowl of soup!

There is an interesting comment made by the writer to the Hebrews on Esau and repentance.

...lest there be any fornicator or profane person like Esau, who for one morsel of food sold his birthright.

For you know that afterward, when he wanted to inherit the blessing, he was rejected, for he found no place for repen - tance, though he sought it diligently with tears.

Hebrews 12:16,17

Later Esau regretted that he had sold the birthright. He tried to regain it and the blessing, but he was rejected. Why? Because he found no place of repentance. In the margin of my *King James Version,* the alternative translation of verse 17 says, "He found no way to change his mind."

Esau cried aloud and shed bitter tears. But he found no place of repentance. By a trivial and impetuous act, he had decided the whole course of his life and his destiny. He had committed himself to a course from which he could find no way of return. These are very sobering words. You can choose sin, make your commitment, and find that you don't want to change your mind.

A New Testament Example

A classic illustration of repentance is that of the Prodigal Son. Sitting in a pigpen, the Bible says, "He came to himself" (Luke 15:17). Those words are so dramatic. In other words, he simply said to himself, *What am I doing sitting here?* Then he made an inward decision: *I will arise and go to my father* (v. 18).

The Prodigal Son climbed out of the pigpen—probably still stinking like the swine—and walked down the road towards home. When his father saw him afar off, his father ran down the road to welcome him. That young man was going one way, sitting in the pigpen, and then realized, *No, this is wrong. I'm going to stop it.* He stopped, turned, and went in the other direction. That is repentance.

Repentance has a direct bearing on our thought life. When you repent, you start to think differently. Repentance is not an emotion, but a decision. True repentance must always go before true faith. Without true repentance there can never be true faith.

Foundation for Salvation

The writer of Hebrews instructed the Hebrew church about repentance.

> *Leaving the principles of the doctrine of Christ, let us go on unto perfection; not laying again the foundation of repen - tance from dead works, and of faith toward God,*
>
> *Of the doctrine of baptisms, and of laying on of hands, and of resurrection of the dead, and of eternal judgment.*
>
> Hebrews 6:1,2

We see in this passage that repentance from dead works is the first foundational doctrine of the Christian faith. The Gospels tell us, "John did...preach the baptism of repentance for the remission of sins" (Mark 1:4).

Notice some of the first words that Jesus spoke as He entered the ministry:

> *The time is fulfilled, and the kingdom of God is at hand: repent ye, and believe the gospel.*
>
> Mark 1:15 KJV

This indicates that "repent ye" is the foundation for salvation. A person cannot believe the Gospel until he repents first.

Another example that bears this out occurred on the Day of Pentecost when Peter preached. The people were pricked in their hearts by his message and asked, "Men and brethren, what shall we do?" (Acts 2:37 KJV). Remember, Peter's first word in answering their question was "repent."

*Peter said unto them, Repent, and be baptized every one
of you in the name of Jesus Christ for the remission of sins,
and ye shall receive the gift of the Holy Ghost.*

Acts 2:38 KJV

See also Paul's farewell address to the Ephesian elders at Troas:

*How I kept back nothing that was helpful, but proclaimed
it to you, and taught you publicly and from house to house,*

*Testifying to Jews, and also to Greeks, repentance toward
God and faith toward our Lord Jesus Christ.*

Acts 20:20,21

The order of Paul's message is consistent. First repentance,
then faith.

Paul also preached to the philosophers on Mars Hill saying,

God commands all men everywhere to repent.

Acts 17:30

Every gospel preacher in the Bible preached this one foundational message—repentance toward our God and faith toward our
Lord Jesus Christ. Faith will be an empty profession and there will be
instability and insecurity in a person's walk with God until there is a
thorough understanding of repentance.

True or Counterfeit?

In 1 Corinthians 5 Paul sharply rebuked the church for a man
who was practicing incest. The church responded to his rebuke by
obeying Paul's instruction. They were sorrowful when they realized

that the sin had been allowed in their church. So Paul wrote again to comfort them.

> *Though I made you sorry with a letter, I do not repent, though I did repent: for I perceive that the same epistle hath made you sorry, though it were but for a season.*
>
> *Now I rejoice, not that ye were made sorry, but that ye sorrowed to repentance: for ye were made sorry after a godly manner, that ye might receive damage by us in nothing.*
>
> *For godly sorrow worketh repentance to salvation not to be repented of: but the sorrow of the world worketh death.*
>
> 2 Corinthians 7:8–10 KJV

There is a true repentance and a counterfeit repentance, and many people don't know how to determine which is which. But the Bible explains it clearly right here. There is a godly sorrow that leads to godly repentance. But there is another kind of sorrow as well. Esau had that. He cried bitterly with remorse, but couldn't find a place of repentance though he sought it with tears. The passage above refers to this kind of repentance as "the sorrow of the world."

It is vital that when we come under conviction of the Holy Spirit, we are able to determine if we have a godly sorrow or if it is simply remorse—feeling embarrassed that we were caught in sin, feeling bad about the sin, but not making a decision to turn around and stop it.

Been There, Done That

Paul probably understood repentance better than anyone. In Acts 26, he described his actions prior to being born again, stating that he not only put many saints into prison, he also voted to have them put to death. He even went so far as to compel them to blaspheme. (See Acts 26:10–12.) Paul (known as Saul before he repented) was about as anti-Christ as a man could be.

One day Saul had an encounter with the Lord on the road to Damascus and was blinded for three days. Can you imagine the images imprinted on his mind in those three days of blindness? It was like watching a video in his imagination. He must have seen and heard the screams of the little children as he pulled their mothers away. He must have heard the sound of bones being broken as stones were hurled at Stephen, killing him. He must have recalled the hatred in his heart and his self-righteous attitude as he thought, *You heretic, how can you declare that Jesus is our Messiah?*

But all that changed on the Damascus road. Saul experienced godly sorrow and became Paul, the apostle of Jesus Christ. When he told us about repentance in 2 Corinthians, chapter 7, he knew what he was talking about. He had been there and done that and bought the T-shirt. He knew from experience that godly sorrow produces repentance, a change of mind.

The Sorrow of the World

Paul also spoke of "the sorrow of the world," which "worketh death" (2 Cor. 7:10). The story of the Last Supper in Matthew 26 relates an excellent illustration, contrasting the two types of sorrow. Two men that night were going to repent after the meal. One of them would betray Jesus; the other would deny Him. But they all dipped their fingers in the same bowl with Him at the dinner table.

As they were sitting around the table, Jesus said, "He that dippeth his hand with me in the dish, the same shall betray me" (v. 23 KJV), and then went on to make this powerful statement:

> *"Woe unto that man by whom the Son of man is betrayed!*
> *it had been good for that man if he had not been born."*

Immediately Judas asked Him, "Master, is it I?"

Jesus replied, "Thou hast said."

That night Judas sold his Master for thirty pieces of silver. According to Matthew 27:3-5, later Judas went back to the high priest, wanting to return the money and undo what he had done. But the chief priests wouldn't take the money.

> *Then Judas, which had betrayed him, when he saw that he was condemned, repented himself, and brought again the thirty pieces of silver to the chief priests and elders,*
>
> *Saying, I have sinned in that I have betrayed the innocent blood. And they said, What is that to us? see thou to that.*
>
> *And he cast down the pieces of silver in the temple, and departed, and went and hanged himself.*

The *King James Version* here says that Judas "repented himself." Another Bible translation says, "He was remorseful." The Greek word for "remorseful" is very close to the word for repentance— *metanoein*. It is *metamelomai,*[3] which means Judas cried or had severe anguish and severe sorrow for what he had done. This translation says he repented.

He tried to repent, but it was the sorrow of the world, meaning he was sorry that there was no way to undo it. He couldn't repent with godly sorrow, even though he tried to with tears, and he ended up going out and hanging himself.

This account of Judas's betrayal and remorse illustrates the sorrow of the world, which leads to bitterness and hardness toward God and ultimately death in some form.

The Other Kind of Sorrow

There was another man who dipped His fingers in the bowl. Jesus told the disciples that He was going to have to die the next day. But Peter said, "Though all men shall be offended because of thee, yet will I never be offended" (Matt. 26:33 KJV). In other words, "I don't care if everybody else forsakes you; I won't." Peter was the "foot-in-the-mouth" disciple, and he basically opened his mouth to change feet.

After Judas betrayed Jesus and the soldiers took Him away, "Peter followed him afar off" (v. 58). You no doubt know the rest of the story. Peter denied that he knew Jesus three times. To really get the full understanding, however, you have to look a little deeper into what the passage says in the Greek.

In verse 74, it states, "[Peter] began to curse and to swear, saying, I know not the man." In essence he was saying, "May God smite me dead right now if I'm telling you a lie," yet he was lying through his teeth.

No sooner had those words come out of his mouth than the rooster crowed. All four Gospels say that Peter went out and wept bitterly. The book of Luke, however, gives us some additional insight. After Peter cursed and swore, Luke 22:61 KJV states, "The Lord turned, and looked upon Peter."

What do you think was in His look? I believe it was forgiveness. That one look from Jesus took the heart of the big fisherman and squeezed it like a sponge, and then Peter went out into the night and wept like a baby.

Again, there were two kinds of repentance that night. Judas had one, and Peter had the other. Similarly, Esau had the sorrow of the world, and David had godly sorrow.

Repentance Can Be Abused

The problem with repentance is that it can be abused so easily. Our churches are full of people who come and repent on Sunday, then live like the devil all week because they think they can do it and get away with it by repenting the next Sunday.

There's an incredible illustration of this in Phil Yancey's book, *What's So Amazing About Grace?* He talks about a convict on a maximum security island, who one day suddenly killed a fellow prisoner and showed no remorse whatsoever.[4] When the bewildered judge asked why he had done it, the prisoner replied, "I was sick of life on the island...and saw no reason to live."

The judge asked him why he hadn't just drowned himself.

The man said, "I'm a Catholic. If I commit suicide, I'll go straight to hell. But if I murder, I can...confess to a priest before my execution. That way, God will forgive me."

What a grisly example this is of the perverted logic of a mind that experiences remorse but not true repentance.

Will You Want To Repent Afterward?

Another dramatic story that Phil Yancey tells is of a man he calls Daniel who was sitting with him in a restaurant late one night.[5] Daniel told him, "I'm going to leave my wife. After fifteen years of a good marriage, I have found a younger, prettier woman. She makes me feel alive."

He had no problem trading in his first wife as if he were trading in a car. He was a Christian, and he knew the moral consequences of what he was doing. He knew he was going to damage his wife and three wonderful children, but his new "love" was too strong to resist.

Daniel asked Phil, "Do you think God can forgive something as awful as what I am about to do?"

Yancey said silence lasted through three cups of coffee with the question lying on the table like a live snake.

Finally Yancey responded. "How do you know that you'll want to repent if you go ahead with this course of action?" In other words, how do you know you will want to repent after the fact?

Subsequently, Daniel went his own way with no repentance. He rationalized, "God is not a part of my life right now. Maybe later."

Jude 4 talks about men who change the grace of God into a license for immorality. But Jesus said in John 6:44 KJV, "No man can come to me except the Father which hath sent me draw him." Repentance is a gift from God. It is something you do, but you do it in response to action that God has initiated.

Repentance is not a condition of God's love and forgiveness. God loves you and forgives you before you ever repent. So you don't win His love and forgiveness because you repent; you don't buy anything by repenting. It is not an act of works that gains the favor. Repentance is simply a route that brings you into the love and manifestation of His grace.

Let me repeat—true repentance is an inner change of mind resulting in an outward turning around to face a completely new direction. God speaks to us from His Word and says to "bring your thoughts into captivity." The Word convicts us and says, "Change your mind. *You can choose to think differently.*" This is an act of grace—an invitation from the Holy Spirit that is meant to bring us into the blessings of God. Repentance is not a negative word; it is the doorway to real faith.

CHAPTER 3

"What Is It About This Book?"—The Word

In Chapter 1 I mentioned the three primary areas of thought attack: 1) temptation, 2) deception, and 3) accusation. God obviously knows how Satan wants to attack us and consequently has given us three weapons that deal directly with these attacks. The three weapons are: The Word, the Name, and the Blood.

The Word of God is the direct conqueror of temptation. The name of Jesus is the antidote to deception. The blood of Jesus defeats all satanic thoughts of accusation. Let me say it again—we must become experts in using our weapons. So let's look at each weapon separately, beginning in this chapter with the Word.

The Bible is no ordinary book. Referred to as the "sword of the Spirit" in Ephesians 6:17, the Word of God is the weapon He has given us to fight temptation. The three foundational temptations of Satan are the lust of the flesh, the lust of the eyes, and the pride of life. First John 2:15-16 says, "Do not love the world or the things in the world. If anyone loves the world, the love of the Father is not in him. For all that is in the world—the lust of the flesh, the lust of the eyes, and the pride of life—is not of the Father but is of the world." Those are the three temptations that Satan gave Adam and Eve in the

Garden. They saw that the tree was good for food (lust of the flesh), that it was pleasant to the eyes (lust of the eyes), and a tree desirable to make one wise (pride of life).

Jesus had to deal with the same three temptations in the wilderness when the devil tempted Him: to turn a stone into bread—1) lust of flesh; to jump off the top of the temple because the angels would lift Him up—2) pride of life; and to receive the kingdoms of the world by bowing down and worshiping Satan (Matt. 4:1-10)—3) lust of the eyes.

The three aspects of temptation that Satan suggested to Adam and Eve were also suggested to Jesus. The temptations Jesus defeated include the nature of all temptation itself. Every temptation falls under one of the three headings.

The power of temptation in our lives depends directly on the thought strongholds that we have developed over the years. These temptations fall into the three categories named above.

The Lust of the Flesh—this appeals to our physical appetites and their gratification. With Adam and Eve it was the fruit, with Jesus it was bread, with us it may be sex, food, leisure, or excess comfort—wherever you are vulnerable in your physical appetites.

The Lust of the Eyes—we see what the world has to offer and we crave it over our personal relationship with God. Television tells us we need it, so we believe we have to have it. We end up trying to manipulate God's will in our lives. We demand that God respond to our wishes. We ask Him to prove Himself to us.

The Pride of Life—Satan told Eve that if she ate the forbidden fruit she would become like God. This is the first New Age lie. You rule your own world. Satan offered Jesus the kingdoms of the world—same thing. You don't need God anymore. You don't need to worship Him and seek His direction.

Notice that Jesus said, "It is written," to answer every temptation. He used the Word of God as a weapon.

What do we mean when we say "the Word of God"? Obviously, this is a very basic question, but it is vital to our understanding of this powerful weapon.

The apostle John received revelation on the Word and shared it with us in John 1.

In the beginning was the Word, and the Word was with God, and the Word was God.

And the Word became flesh, and dwelt among us, and we beheld His glory, the glory as of the only begotten of the Father, full of grace and truth.

John 1:1,14

Who was John talking about in these verses? Of course, he was talking about Jesus—Jesus Christ is the Word of God. But no doubt you have noticed that time and again we refer to the Bible as the Word of God.

*The **word** of God is living and powerful, and sharper than any two-edged sword, piercing even to the division of* *soul and spirit, and of joints and marrow, and is a discerner of the thoughts and intents of the heart.*

Hebrews 4:12

So which is it? Is Jesus Christ the Word of God, or is the Bible the Word of God?

The answer to that question is profound. If we do not understand the answer, we cannot approach the Word in faith. Is Jesus the Word of God? Yes, He is. Is the Bible the Word of God? Yes, it is. They are both the Word. But how can the Bible and Jesus be the same thing?

Living Word and Written Word

Jesus is the *living* Word, and the Bible is the *written* Word. In essence, in character, and in content, they are one and the same. They both manifest God to us. As we will see, the very same energizing life principle found in Jesus is also contained in the pages of your Bible.

Unfortunately, many people do not understand this. For example, I know that if your pastor were to announce that Jesus Christ was going to be at your church next Sunday morning for a healing service, you would be there. And there is no doubt that if Jesus showed up and laid hands on you that you would be healed.

Yet, a large majority of Christians doubt they will be healed when the Word of God is preached. We expect power demonstrations from Jesus but not from the Scripture. We in the church have been playing childish and foolish games, and that is where we miss it. We would expect healing from Jesus Himself, but we do not expect it from His Word.

The Word Became Flesh

According to John 1:1, "In the beginning was the Word, and the Word was with God, and the Word was God." The Word was God. God and His Word are one. When Jesus came He was the Word of God becoming flesh. So we can truthfully say that *Jesus is the Word of God;* but *the Bible is also the Word of God.* To confirm this point, let's refer to the Greek word translated "word."

John 1 uses the term "word" in verse 1, which is translated from the Greek word *logos*.[1] With that in mind, look again at Hebrews 4:12.

*The **word** of God is living and powerful, and sharper than any two-edged sword, piercing even to the division of soul and spirit, and of joints and marrow, and is a discerner of the thoughts and intents of the heart.*

This verse is referring to the Bible, God's written Word. The Greek translation of "word" here is the same word used in John 1—*logos*.[2] The point we can derive from these verses is that the Bible and Jesus are both the *logos*, the Word of God. They are one and the same in essence and power.

Full of Life

Jesus, the living Word, is full of the same life as the Word of God (the Bible).

In Him [Jesus] was life, and the life was the light of men.

John 1:4

The word "life" in this verse is taken from the Greek word *zoe*,[3] which means the absolute fullness of life that belongs to God.[4] That is divine life; it's God's life. *Zoe* is what God is; it's His nature, His substance. *Zoe* is the essence of God and the essence of His Son Jesus. The essence of Jesus—His life—is *zoe*.

Remember, this very same *zoe,* or the God kind of life that is found in Jesus Christ, is also found in the pages of your Bible. Jesus tried to explain it to the disciples in John 6:63 KJV.

> *The words that I speak unto you, they are spirit, and they are life.*

The word "life" in this verse is the same word for life used in John 1:4—*zoe*.[5] By this we can see that the words that Jesus spoke in the Word of God contain the same life that is in Jesus Himself. Another way we could say it is that your Bible, the Word of God, contains the same life—the same intense vibrant energy and activity—that is in Jesus.

Notice in John 6:63 that Jesus also said about His words, "They are *spirit*." The word "spirit" here is taken from the Greek word *pneuma*.[6] Jesus only spoke God's words (John 14:10 TLB), so you could say that God's Word is spirit.

Two chapters earlier in John 4:24 KJV, Jesus said, "*God* is a Spirit." The word "Spirit" here is also taken from the Greek word *pneuma*.[7] Since God and Jesus are one, we could say that Jesus is a Spirit.

If the above statements are true, and I believe they are, then we can say Jesus and God's Word are both Spirit, they are both alive—and they are equally as powerful.

The same power that is found in Jesus is also found in the written Scriptures.

"What Is This?"

When I was in Afghanistan in June 2002, a pastor there told me a story. One day an elder from a refugee camp came to his church and asked for a Bible in the Pashtun language. He gave him a Bible, and a week later the elder came back very agitated.

He said, "Sir, what is it about this book?"

The pastor replied, "What do you mean?"

The elder said, "Every time I open the book, I see a vision of a Lamb standing by a glorious throne in front of millions and millions of people. What is this? When I close the book, it goes away. When I open it up, it comes back. What is this?"

The pastor turned to Revelation 5 and read him the entire chapter about Jesus, the Lamb who was slain standing before the throne of God, surrounded by millions worshiping Him.

The man broke down and wept. He said, "That's what I see every time I open the book. What is this?" The pastor then led this man to Jesus.

The pastor told me, "When you go back to the West, tell people that Jesus is appearing in refugee camps." We hear the same thing coming from the Middle East. Jesus is appearing to people there. A large percentage of those being born again in the Middle East are having visions of Jesus.

That is awesome when you think about it.

God is doing something sovereign in the Muslim world. Jesus is appearing to people in visions. Others see Jesus in the written Word. It just proves to me that the Bible is a living book. Through it God comes to us in the form of words, and those words are Spirit and they are life.

The Same Power

Peter put it this way:

> *According as his divine power hath given unto us all things that pertain unto life and godliness, through the knowledge of him that hath called us to glory and virtue:*
>
> *Whereby are given unto us exceeding great and precious promises: that by these ye might be partakers of the divine nature, having escaped the corruption that is in the world through lust.*

2 Peter 1:3,4 KJV

The word "life" in verse 3 is also the Greek word *zoe*[8]—the same life that Jesus has. Notice it says that He has given us "all things" that pertain to *zoe*. "All things" includes healing, righteousness, blessings, finances, and anything else that pertains to your life. God has given you everything you could ever need; legally, it is yours.

So how do you possess these things? It is through His "exceeding great and precious promises" that we partake of His divine nature. I like to say it like this: In the Old Testament God led Joshua into the Promised Land; in the New Testament, Jesus leads believers into the land of promises!

I believe that when I put God's Word, His promises, on my lips, under the anointing of the Holy Spirit, the same life of God continues to energize those words. I believe that when I preach God's Word regarding healing to you, God will heal you, because the healing power is in His words. It is amazing that there is the same healing power in Jesus of Nazareth that there is in your Bible. It is the same power. It is the same energy. It is the same life—*zoe*.

Having a revelation of this will change the way you approach reading your Bible. Your faith has to put a demand on God's Word and expect those words to come alive—expect those words to heal, expect those words to bless your marriage, expect those words to touch your business and turn your finances around. That is why God gave us His Word. His Word is alive and it contains answers for every problem we face. Our part is to believe that the *zoe* in God's Word truly is our daily bread.

Mary's Story

Some years ago I was preaching in Winnipeg, Manitoba, Canada, and we were experiencing a heavy snowstorm. It was about twenty below zero, so I spent a lot of time inside. As I was praying and studying the Christmas story in the Bible, the Lord opened up some things to me regarding it that I knew were revelations. You may have never heard the story of Mary in quite this way.

The angel Gabriel was sent from God unto a city of Galilee, named Nazareth,

To a virgin espoused to a man whose name was Joseph, of the house of David; and the virgin's name was Mary.

And the angel came in unto her, and said, Hail, thou that art highly favoured, the Lord is with thee: blessed art thou among women.

...thou hast found favour with God.

And, behold, thou shalt conceive in thy womb, and bring forth a son, and shalt call his name Jesus.

He shall be great, and shall be called the Son of the Highest....

Then said Mary unto the angel, How shall this be, seeing I know not a man?

And the angel answered and said unto her, The Holy Ghost shall come upon thee, and the power of the Highest shall overshadow thee: therefore also that holy thing which shall be born of thee shall be called the Son of God.

For with God nothing shall be impossible.

And Mary said, Behold the handmaid of the Lord; be it unto me according to thy word. And the angel departed from her.

Luke 1:26–28;30–32;34,35;37;38 KJV

Let's imagine the scene in heaven before Gabriel appeared to Mary. It probably went something like this: God called Gabriel to the throne and said, "Gabriel, the time for Messiah has arrived. I want you to carry My spoken word to a young virgin in Nazareth named Mary."

The angel said, "Yes, Father," then flew out of heaven carrying one thing: the Word of God on his lips.

Most likely, Mary was a teenage girl when the angel appeared to her. In that day, it was customary for a young woman to be betrothed at sixteen or seventeen. We read that this young woman was in her home in Nazareth, when suddenly there was a blinding flash of light. A large angel, Gabriel, appeared in her home and said to her, "Hail, you that are highly favored among women. The Lord is with you. The power of the Most High will overshadow you. That which is conceived in your womb will be called the Son of the Highest."

Mary was shocked. She backed away from the angel and said, "But how can these things be? I am a virgin. I know not a man."

The answer the angel gave Mary has almost been lost to us in the *King James Version,* but I want you to see this because it is powerful. In verse 37, the angel said to Mary, "With God nothing shall be impossible." The word "nothing" in the Greek can actually be translated as two words: no *rhema,* or no word."[9]

Rhema and Logos

Both *rhema* and *logos* are Greek words that are translated "the Word of God," but *logos* has a greater context. *Logos* refers to the Word of God in its entirety, from Genesis to Revelation. It is the inspired, eternal Word of God that is forever settled in heaven.

The word *rhema* means "a word that is spoken." It is the word used when God takes a part of the whole Bible and speaks it to you under the anointing of the Holy Spirit. It is the word *rhema* that appears in Romans 10:17: "Faith comes by hearing, and hearing by the word [*rhema*] of God."[10] Jesus used *rhema* when He said, "'Man shall not live by bread alone, but by every word [*rhema*] that proceeds from the mouth of God'" (Matt. 4:4).[11]

Have you ever been reading the Bible when all of a sudden, even though you had read a verse a hundred times, on that particular day the verse leapt off the page and burned a hole in your heart? It came alive. You saw it in a way that you had never seen it before. It touched you. It ministered to you. The Holy Spirit spoke a *rhema* to your spirit.

When the angel said to Mary, "With God nothing shall be impossible," literally the angel was saying, "With God, no *rhema* shall be impossible." Notice this is a double negative. If we turn it around to the positive, the angel was saying, "Mary, every word that God speaks, every *rhema* of God will be possible."

The *American Standard Version* says it this way: "No word from God shall be void of power" (Luke 1:37). A more free translation is "every word that God speaks contains the power in the word itself, for its own fulfillment."

Mary received a revelation of this; she saw it. She probably thought to herself, *Oh, that's how I will get pregnant.* What did she say to the angel? "Be it unto me according to thy word" (Luke 1:38 KJV). Instantly Mary was made pregnant by her faith responding to the seed of the Word of God.

Hook Your Faith Up With the Word

Many discount Mary because she has been exalted in an exaggerated way through religion. But we can learn a great deal from her. She was not a robot being dictated to by an angel and being told, "You do not have a choice. You are going to bear Jesus whether you like it or not." No, Mary had to agree to the proposition. Her faith had to hook up with the Word of God. She had to receive it, and she did.

The angel spoke over her and said, "The power of the Highest shall overshadow you," and she said to the angel, "But how? How can I, a young woman that has never known a man, bear a child?"

The angel said, "Mary, the Word that I've already spoken over you has the power in itself for its own fulfillment. The power to make you pregnant, Mary, is in the Word of God that I have delivered to you."

How did she respond to the angel? She said, "Be it unto me according to thy word." Her faith hooked up with the Word from God. The spoken Word came down from heaven, carried by an angel. It connected with Mary's faith, and by faith the spoken Word of heaven became the living Word, Jesus, in her womb: "The Word became flesh" (John 1:14).

That is what happens when you carry the Word of God on your lips to people. You carry life. You carry authority. You carry the mighty power of God Himself.

In 1978 my music group, *Living Sound,* and I took our first trip into Russia at the prompting of the Holy Spirit. We were driving from Finland to Leningrad (now St. Petersburg). When we reached the Russian border (a very imposing place filled with guard dogs and machine guns), we were stopped and searched.

Soon a Russian guard came over to us waving a fistful of Christian literature he had found in our belongings. I had instructed our team to take all Christian literature off of the bus before this trip, but someone had forgotten the literature under some clothing.

The guard took me down a hall and sat me in a room. He told me I was on my way to a Soviet prison. I waited in that room for four hours. I remember the one word that kept coming out of my mouth was "Father." I needed the protection of the heavenly Father, and that word kept coming to my lips. Then I began praying in the Spirit and quoting God's Word: "God has not given us a spirit of fear, but of power and of love and of a sound [disciplined] mind" (2 Tim. 1:7).

I was kept there for four hours while they checked our Christian literature. In the meantime, I was building my spirit up in the Word of God because I knew I was eventually going to face Soviet interrogators. Finally, I was taken before a Russian general who began to brow beat me, accusing me of being a spy sent by the CIA and telling me I was to go to prison. There was also a guard there holding a machine gun with a bayonet attached. When the general finished yelling at me, he said, "Do you have anything to say?"

I had been quoting the Word under my breath, and I felt the power of God rise up inside of me. I looked at that man and said, "Why are you afraid of me?"

Astonished, he answered, "Afraid of you? Ha! We're not afraid of you."

I said, "Well, why is that soldier standing there with a gun? You've searched me. Do I have a gun?"

"No," he answered.

I continued, "Why is there a bayonet on his rifle? You're afraid of me. In fact, you're terrified of me. I'm sitting here with no weapons. You've searched me."

Again, he insisted, "We're not afraid of you."

I said, "All right, if you're not afraid of me, then you'll let me into Russia."

He said, "Yes, we will."

I said, "Thank you, sir." And that's how we got into that country. I know this sounds exaggerated, but that is the way it happened.

The Word is powerful. It has power to save, heal, deliver, and set people free.

Natural Results

When your pastor stands up Sunday after Sunday and delivers the Word of God to your church, there are sinners who say, "Pastor, I hear what you are saying from God's Word. I believe what you say about Jesus Christ. I am willing to repent of my sin."

What happens when a sinner believes the Word regarding salvation? By faith, God's Word is turned into a living Jesus in that person's heart. It is a miracle that happens in many churches Sunday after Sunday after Sunday. The Word becomes flesh and comes to live in our flesh. It is the power of the incarnation being repeated again.

This is why, when I preach the Word to the sick, it is not Terry Law who heals anybody. It is the Word of God that has the character of life and healing in it. My faith must put a demand for healing on that Word and say, "Lord, Your healing is here. It is in the Word." I have to become like Mary and say, "Be it unto me according to Your Word."

If your faith will believe it and if you will receive it, what can happen? You can be healed, because that is the natural result of the Word of God. It naturally heals. That is its character, its essence, its nature—to heal. "He sent His Word and healed them, and delivered them from their destructions" (Ps. 107:20).

The Sword of the Spirit

I have seen demons do exactly what I tell them to do when I quote them the Word of God. They respect the power that is there. When Jesus met the devil in the wilderness, how did He oppose him? He said three words: "It is written" (Matt. 4:4). Jesus took the Word of God and told the devil what God had to say about the matter.

In Ephesians 6:17 the Word of God is referred to as "the sword of the Spirit." If you do not believe that verse, if you do not commit yourself to that Word, if you do not demand by faith that the Word work in your life, the Holy Spirit has no sword to work with. You have taken it away from Him.

The Holy Spirit would say to each one of us, "Pick up that Word." Like Jesus, when you face the devil in the wilderness of negative circumstances, say, "Get out of here, Satan!" (See Matt. 4:10 NLT.) Why? Because "It is written," and the Word, through your faith, becomes a powerful weapon against the temptations of the enemy.

We saw earlier that when the devil approached Eve in the Garden, he said three words, "Hath God said?" (Gen. 3:1 KJV). That was the question that introduced sin to the human race, the three words that brought the curse upon us all.

"Has God said?" Yes, God *has* said! Remember, when Satan tempted Jesus, Jesus' reply was, "It is written," because Jesus remembered what God had said. He knew there was life in God's Word, and He knew the devil had to bow to the Word. When the devil heard "It is written," he was silenced.

How about you? Where is your faith concerning the Word? Are you believing for God's Word to come alive in you? Do you believe that the Word will bring life when you speak it to an unsaved, unbelieving friend or loved one?

In 1 Peter 1:23, the Bible says, "We were born again, not of corruptible [perishable][12] seed, but of the incorruptible [immortal][13] seed of the Word of God." There is life in the Word—life for faith, life for the new birth, life for spiritual food, healing, prosperity and abundance, life for victory over the devil, life for spiritual cleansing by the washing of the water of the Word. (See Eph. 5:26.) The Word is a mirror we look into. It is our light. David said, "Your word is a lamp to my feet and a light to my path" (Ps. 119:105).

For years many believers have given lip service to the Bible, but their faith has never believed that the Word was alive. But this Word has to come alive in our hearts if we are going to live victoriously. It is one of the spiritual weapons that God has given the body of Christ. If we will get a revelation of this, we will see people get healed when we pray for them. We can see disease removed from human bodies. We can see a manifestation of the glory of God. The power of God's Word will do it.

Get Into the Good Fight

In 1 Timothy 6:12, Paul exhorts Timothy, "Fight the good fight of faith." Notice that God is not asking us to fight *the devil*. We are told to fight the good fight "of faith." God never said it would be easy, and there's definitely a fight involved. You fight to put God's words in your mouth when thought attacks endeavor to pull you down. You're fighting the good fight of faith as you take God's Word and apply it against the enemy.

To illustrate, we read what God told Joshua in Joshua 1:3: "Every place that the sole of your foot will tread upon [future] I have given you [past]." In other words, every place that you're going to walk in the future has already been given to you, but it won't be yours until you walk it out.

This is where many people misunderstand faith. God told Joshua that the land was theirs. Joshua could have stood there on the bank of the Jordan River and said, "Hallelujah, I've got it all. God says it's mine, and I am just going to stand here and thank God that I have it."

But God said, "Every place that your feet are going to tread in the future is yours. I've already given it to you, but you have to walk it out before it becomes yours."

Everything in God is yours. It is all in the life of God, and you have His life inside you when you are born again. But we are commanded to enter the land of the giants and start walking out our faith. That's the good fight of faith.

Walking It Out

I remember one special time when I had to walk out my faith and go in and occupy the land. It was a time when the Lord asked me to go somewhere I didn't want to go. I was in Cyprus on vacation in the summer of 2002 when someone mentioned to me that Lebanon was only 125 miles away. As I was thinking about how close Cyprus was to the Middle East, I felt the Holy Spirit say in my heart, "I want you to go to the Middle East."

At first I argued with Him. "Lord, I haven't been there for twenty-five years. The only thing I hear about is the suicide bombings and killings. I have no contacts of any kind in the Middle East."

Suddenly, Joshua 1:3 came back to me concerning the Lord giving us the land. I remembered that if we will walk it out, "Every place that the sole of your foot will tread upon I have given you, as I said to Moses." I sensed the Lord was saying to me, "Get over there and watch what I'll do." So that very day I called my ministry office and asked them to make the travel arrangements. That's how important I believe the Word of God is. We must act on it immediately.

A few months later, in December 2002 (which was three months before the Iraq war started), I left on a fact-finding mission to several cities in the Middle East (Cairo, Beirut, Amman, Damascus, and Jerusalem), visiting with Christian leaders to find out what God was doing in their areas.

While in Jordan I met a young Arab named Nabil who mentioned that his wife came from Iraq. As soon as he said "Iraq" the Spirit of the Lord whispered inside me, "That's why you're here," and I knew I would be going to Iraq. It had not occurred to me until that moment that I'd be going there. I believe it was happening because I was walking out what God had told me to do—"enter the land of the giants and start walking out your faith." That's the good fight of faith.

Nabil also told me that his father-in-law, George Sada, was a retired air force officer. He used to fly airplanes for Saddam Hussein and knew him personally. He talked Saddam out of bombing Israel with chemical weapons in 1991. He had been a two-star general in the Iraqi Air Force (he retired from the military before the first Gulf War and never fought against America). The most important thing was that he was a born-again Christian.

Before I realized what I was saying, I asked, "Can your father-in-law get me into Baghdad?" Nabil called London and talked to George, who said, "I'll call the minister of religion in Baghdad and see what we can find out." Half an hour later, he called us and said, "You're free to go in. It's a miracle. Your visas will be granted in ten days."

At that time American civilians were not allowed on the ground in Iraq. It was illegal for me to go in without being a news or television correspondent of some kind. I called someone I knew at the NBC TV network in Tulsa and got them to hire me for a dollar a year. That enabled me to carry a television identification card and gave me a legal right to be in Iraq.

When I arrived in Baghdad, I saw fear among the people like I had never seen before. While there, I visited Saddam's children's hospital. As I entered the front door, the hospital administrator became very angry when he learned I was American.

"Your people are responsible for the deaths in this hospital," he declared. "Every child in this hospital is dying of leukemia. If we had chemotherapy drugs we could treat 80 percent of them. Your government has embargoed our country for the last twelve years. You have stopped medicine getting to our children. We have lost 500,000 children to disease that could have been cured. You are murderers."

When he said this I was stunned. I was more than stunned; I was embarrassed. I determined to get to the bottom of the accusation to see if it was true.

I subsequently found out, through queries with our government and with the U.N., that during the twelve years of the embargo, the West (including the U.S. and the U.K.) had purchased over 39 billion dollars worth of Iraqi oil, but we didn't purchase it with money. We bought it by paying with food and medicine. It was called the oil-for-food program.

We sent Saddam Hussein $10 billion of the finest American medicine. He sold our medicine on the black market in the Middle East. With the money, he built 68 palaces and prepared himself for war. He allowed 500,000 Iraqi children to die when he had the medicine to treat them. Because he controlled all television broadcasts in the country, he told the Iraqi people that America and the U.K. had killed their children, and for years they didn't know anything different.

When I found this out I said, "Lord, let me go back and show them the truth." The war started on March 19, 2003, and technically it was over shortly thereafter. The President declared it finished on May 1. On May 8, my two sons, Scot and Jason, my associate Joel, and myself decided to go back to Iraq with $80,000 worth of medicine, twelve hundred Arabic Bibles, and thirty-three thousand *Story of Jesus* booklets in Arabic.

The U.S. embassy informed us that they could not give us military escort into Baghdad (the airport was out of commission at that point). They informed us that the only way to Baghdad was over one thousand kilometers of highway—the most dangerous highway in the world. They recommended that we join a convoy.

"There have been five hijackings on that highway in the last two weeks," the embassy said. "The latest was yesterday. The bandits drive up beside you at a high rate of speed and wave a stop sign. If you don't stop for that, they'll wave a machine gun. If you don't stop for that, they'll open fire. They fired sixty rounds into a vehicle yesterday."

As he informed me of the impossibilities of our trip, I prayed quietly. In my spirit I knew I was supposed to go to Baghdad. "Every place that the sole of your foot will tread upon I have given you," Joshua 1:3 says. I knew we could never deliver the medicine without the soles of our feet treading upon the land. So I decided to go.

We joined a convoy of eleven other cars (we had four vehicles of our own). We traveled 100 miles per hour across the desert safely into Baghdad. God protected us.

The first thing we did was to go back to Saddam's children's hospital. We laid our medicine on the floor in front of the administrator's desk. "You accused us of killing your children through the embargo," I said. "We didn't come to kill Iraqi children; we came to heal them in Jesus' name!" Then I told him how Saddam had lied to them about the medicine. I will never forget the look on his face.

Doing God's work is not easy. If we believe for something, then we have to act on God's Word. God has given us the land, but we must walk it out. Paul says, "We walk by faith, and not by sight." (See 2 Cor. 5:7.) In essence, Paul is saying there is a battle involved. We must practice what we preach.

This is the reason it's difficult for some people to believe for their healing or a financial blessing—there is a battle involved. We would rather have evangelists come by, lay their hands on our heads, say a prayer over us, and receive all the blessings that God has for us in that way. We don't want to have to fight the good fight of faith with God's Word.

God may very well use an evangelist as one of His messengers, but if it doesn't happen that way, don't be discouraged. Don't say God doesn't want to heal you or bless you financially. Instead, go to the Word and receive your blessing. Make up your mind to go after it.

Approach the Word

When you approach Scripture, first approach it as being God's Word speaking to you, not words of human wisdom. Paul put it this way:

> For this cause also thank we God without ceasing, because, when ye received the word of God which ye heard of us, ye received it not as the word of men, but as it is in truth, the word of God, which effectually worketh also in you that believe.
>
> 1 Thessalonians 2:13 KJV

The second way to approach God's Word is with meekness:

Therefore lay aside all filthiness and overflow of wicked -
ness, and receive with meekness the implanted word, which is
able to save your souls.

James 1:21

Notice, if you want God's Word to work for you, you must lay
aside all filthiness and overflow of wickedness. Filthiness denotes a
sinful delight in that which is immoral and impure. This attitude
closes the mind and heart against the saving influence of God's Word.
Overflow of naughtiness or wickedness suggests the bad behavior of
a child. Children are "naughty" when they refuse to accept instruction
from their parents and argue with them instead.

Receiving God's Word with meekness means to acknowledge
that God is the Teacher and you are the pupil. Don't superimpose
your doctrine on the Scripture when you read it. Come to the Bible as
a student on your knees, expecting God to bring fresh truth to your
heart. Humbly allow Him to manage your life and teach you.

God's Thoughts

Notice what Isaiah 55:8–11 KJV says about God's Word:

"My thoughts are not your thoughts, neither are your
ways My ways," says the Lord.

"For as the heavens are higher than the earth, so are
My ways higher than your ways, and My thoughts than
your thoughts.

"For as the rain comes down, and the snow from heaven,
and do not return there, but water the earth, and make it

*bring forth and bud, that it may give seed to the sower and
bread to the eater:*

*"So shall My word be that goes forth out of My mouth; it
shall not return to Me void, but it shall accomplish what I
please, and it shall prosper in the thing for which I sent it."*

God's thoughts are up in heaven and our thoughts are carnal
down here on the earth. How do we get God's thoughts from heaven
down into our hearts so we will begin thinking and believing the way
God does?

Notice the phrase, "goeth forth out of my mouth." Every time this
phrase is used (either the exact wording or a statement inferring this),
it is talking about *rhema,* the spoken word. The Greek word *rhema*
simply means "a word that is spoken." So it is associated with the
mouth of God. We see a similar phrase in Matthew 4:4: "'Man shall
not live by bread alone, but by every word [*rhema*] that proceeds
from the mouth of God.'"

We need to understand one of the great guiding principles that is
established in Scripture. God's Word and God's Spirit always work
together in perfect harmony.

David said in Psalm 33:6, "By the word of the Lord the heavens
were made, and all the host of them by the breath of His mouth." The
word "breath" in this verse comes from the Hebrew word for
"spirit."[14] Notice, "The heavens were made and all the host of them"
by two things: 1) the Word of the Lord, and 2) the breath ("Spirit") of
His mouth.

Do you see the picture? As God speaks His Word, His Spirit,
which is His breath, goes with it.

When we say something, our breath leaves our mouth as we pronounce the words. You can't speak without breathing. So it is with God. When He speaks His Word, His Spirit, or breath, goes forth at the same time. God's Word and God's Spirit always work together. When you unite God's Word and God's Spirit in your life, you speak forth the creative power of God.

Let's go back to the passage in Joshua 1:8 that says, "This Book of the Law shall not depart from your mouth." Again, this is referring to the spoken word.

Now back to Isaiah 55:8-11. Isaiah compares the *rhema* word from heaven coming down to earth like the rain or the snow. It comes to water the earth so it will be fertile and bud. When the earth does this, it gives seed to the sower and bread to the eater. What power there is in God's *rhema* word! It will bring abundance to you.

It is important to notice that the initiative always starts with God. It is the Holy Spirit who speaks a *rhema* word of healing into your life. But when it comes, it has God's almighty power in it.

The *rhema* word from God that you need may also come when the pastor is ministering. It may come while you are sitting quietly at home studying Scripture. But when it comes, if you will mix faith with it, God's Word will become that mighty sword to defeat the enemy, and your life will be changed.

Let me say it one more time: "The Word of God is living and powerful" (Heb. 4:12). The Greek word translated "powerful," is *energes,* which also refers to energetic.[15] The idea conveyed to us is that God's Word is full of intense, vibrant energy and activity. It works effectively for those who believe.

What is it about this Book? It is the power of God unto salvation, healing, deliverance, prosperity, and all heavenly blessings.

I challenge you to pick up God's Word as though it were a new book, a book of God's life and power and authority. Believe His Word, trust in what He says, and have confidence in His promises. Then, when you face the thought attack of the enemy who tempts you to sin, you can declare in faith, "It is written!" And the devil will flee from you just as he fled from Jesus.

CHAPTER 4

Tap Into Divine Power, Part 1— The Name of Jesus

I can still remember the thoughts that went through my mind on September 11, 2001. As television images of burning, falling towers raced around the globe, all of us knew that the world would never be the same again.

Shortly after the tragedy, in early October 2001, I sat in my living room watching television. The coalition of nations had declared war on the Taliban in Afghanistan. The war was in progress, and I watched widows and children flee from the fighting.

Words came to my spirit that I had heard in the past, "Do you want to curse the darkness, or do you want to light a candle?" The answer was obvious. I knew that I wanted to light a candle, but I didn't quite know how.

Then the Holy Spirit began to impress upon me very forcibly that I had to get on an airplane and fly to the war zone. I protested vigorously. I didn't know anyone in that part of the world. One week later I found myself on the borders of Afghanistan. Our ministry, World Compassion, felt led of the Lord to minister to widows and orphans in the refugee camps.

I will never forget the looks on the faces of the mothers and children as we put warm jackets on the bodies of the children. The temperature would go down to minus thirteen degrees centigrade at night.

In April 2002 we decided to take a load of food into Southern Afghanistan, in the region of the city of Kandahar. I met an Afghan warlord named Haji. He wanted me to see the terrible straits of the people in his town. We drove rapidly along a Southern Afghan highway, then suddenly he turned into the ditch, and we began to travel across the open desert. It was barren sand, like something you'd expect to see in Saudi Arabia. There were camels and people dressed in long flowing robes.

Haji was driving a Toyota Landcruiser at a speed of about 70 miles per hour. As we drove across the desert, he informed me that the car we were traveling in had been taken from the Taliban in hand-to-hand fighting in Kandahar a couple of months earlier.

I asked him a question: "Did you kill anybody in the battle of Kandahar?" His response surprised me.

He said, "Yes, many people."

I said, "How many?"

He said, "I've lost count."

I said, "Fifty?"

He said, "Many more."

We were traveling in a particular area where Osama bin Laden used to hunt a few months earlier. I didn't know it at the time, but the land over which we were traveling had many land mines. That explained why Haji was driving 70 miles per hour. If we hit a land mine at that speed, we'd be gone before the explosion caught up with us.

There were five of us in the vehicle. The three men in the back-seat were wild-looking Afghan warriors carrying AK47s in their hands. It was at this point that Haji turned to me and said, "You know, I like you Christians, but I don't like Hindus." I thought that was interesting, so I asked him why.

He said, "Well, the Hindus have 300,000 gods, and I don't like that. I like you Christians because we both have the same God." His words exploded on my consciousness, and for a moment I was stunned. Did I dare open my mouth and say what I really believed? I thought of the machine guns in the back seat.

I was quiet for a moment, and then I sensed the Spirit of God rise up inside of me. I replied, "No, we don't have the same God." Haji was driving, and his head turned swiftly to look at me with his dark, piercing eyes.

"What do you mean we don't have the same God?" he asked.

My reply was very simple. "My God has a Son. How about yours? I believe Jesus is the Son of God."

I will never forget the look in his eyes. They grew as big as saucers. It was almost as though I had physically slapped him across the face. I didn't know if he was going to shoot me, curse me, or tell me to get out and walk. But I knew that I had hit on the key that divides our religion from that of Islam.

There are three major religions in the world that teach there is only one God: Judaism, Islam, and Christianity. What sets Christianity apart is that it declares that God has a Son. His name is Jesus Christ. Not only is He the Son of God, but He is God in the same sense that the Father is.

I've learned over and over again in my travels that Jesus (the name of Jesus) is the stumbling block to anyone who is a non-Christian. The underlying deception in every major religion on the planet outside of Christianity rests on the answer to the question, "Who is Jesus Christ?"

There's an interesting portion of Scripture in Revelation 12:7-9.

"And war broke out in heaven: Michael and his angels fought with the dragon; and the dragon and his angels fought, but they did not prevail, nor was a place found for them in heaven any longer. So the great dragon was cast out, that serpent of old, called the Devil and Satan, who deceives the whole world; he was cast to the earth, and his angels were cast out with him."

Notice verse 9 says that the dragon, the devil, Satan, is called the one "who deceives the whole world."

I have stated earlier in the book that one of the three primary attacks that Satan directs against the thought life of the believer is that he comes with thoughts of deception as the deceiver. (Remember, he also attacks through temptation, which we answer with the Word; and through accusation, which we answer with the blood of Jesus.) Keep in mind that the name of Jesus opposes religious deception as we look at the power in His name in this chapter.

One Road to the Mountaintop

I found Haji's comment to be very revealing. In his mind, the Muslim God (Allah) and the Christian God were the same being. This should bring up a basic question in the mind of any Christian who is endeavoring to serve the Lord: Who is this being called Allah for whom large numbers of individuals are not only willing, but desirous of sacrificing their very life? Are Allah and the Christian God the same being?

One of our major Christian periodicals in America postulated the fact that perhaps they were the same supernatural being. What kind of unseen power motivates young people to push the button on a suicide bomb and send themselves into eternity with a desire to successfully kill Christians and Jews, or infidels, as they are called?

You cannot ignore the name Allah any longer. We're seeing it on television almost every day beamed from Iraq or Afghanistan or Palestine or some other nation in the Middle East. I ask you, is Allah just another name for God? Can it be possible that approximately one billion people who call themselves Muslims are making a mistake?

They believe fervently that they will go to heaven because they pray to Allah five times a day. They fast during the month of Ramadan. They will travel at great expense to Mecca to honor Allah. If you ask them what they believe, they will tell you very simply there's no other way to get to heaven than by believing in Allah. They believe that there is *one sure* way to get to heaven—to die as a martyr in Jihad or holy war on behalf of Allah.

There are those amongst us in America and the West who are politically correct. They believe, and rightly so, that in this land of freedom we should protect the rights of Muslims to worship in a mosque, teach the Koran, and talk to others about what they believe. But I wonder sometimes if we are equally as committed to declare that Christians have a right to inform Muslims that Jesus Christ is the only way to God and to heaven. In fact, the Bible says that no one comes to the Father but by Him. (See John 14:6.)

Let me say it very clearly. Allah is not a mediator between God and men. There is only one Mediator between God and man, and that is the man Christ Jesus. It must be the avowed goal of every Christian to inform Muslims that they must turn from serving Allah and place their faith in Jesus Christ as their Lord and Savior.

Let me try to simplify what I have just said. In a land of freedom like America, we must guarantee the rights of Muslims to be Muslims. They have the right to serve Allah if they should choose. We demonstrated this plurality of religion shortly after 9-11. In the National Cathedral in Washington, Muslim, Jewish, and Christian clergy participated together. A week later in Yankee Stadium, we saw a variety of sheiks, Hindus, Muslims, Jews, Christians, and others gathered together for a similar reason.

We are right to allow freedom of all religions in our land. I am afraid, however, that overseas, especially in the Middle East, our political correctness and our insistence on the rights of all people to worship according to the dictates of their own conscience is seen by many as a manifestation of weakness in the Christian faith. When I go to Iraq or Iran or Afghanistan or Jordan, I have not met many followers of Allah who would be willing to fight for the freedom of others to practice Christianity in their countries.

In the kingdom of God, however, Christians are politically incorrect. Let me say it very clearly. There are no other roads to the top of the mountain. There are no other ways to God. There are no multiple highways to heaven. There is no other name under heaven given among men by which we must be saved, and that name is Jesus. (See Acts 4:12.)

Make no mistake about Allah: he is a spiritual personality, a spiritual being created by our God. He is a fallen angelic being just like

Satan. He was thrown out of heaven by God, along with Satan and a third of the other angels who followed Satan. But he is no more God than Buddha or Lucifer. Allah is one of the angels who made the decision to become a messenger of darkness. (I talk more about this in my book on angels, *The Truth About Angels*.)

Only Creatures, Not the Creator

I remember sitting in a restaurant in Kabul, Afghanistan, talking to a missionary from the West who had worked in Afghanistan for many years. Quietly, I asked him the question, "Who do you think Allah is? Is he the same as the Christian God?"

He looked carefully in several directions, leaned across the table, and whispered, "No, Allah is an evil spirit. He is a demonic being."

What does God think when one billion people He has created decide that they will worship Allah and turn their back upon the Son of God, Jesus Christ? After the great sacrifice God made in sending His Son to this world, what is His response to those who so easily ignore His Son?

Frankly, I believe it makes God angry. The Bible says that the wrath of God is revealed against those who exchange the truth of God for a lie and worship and serve the creature rather than the Creator. (See Rom. 1:18,25.)

I want to say it clearly—Allah is not the Creator; he is a creature. He is only one of 360 deities, all demonic spirits, worshipped by different tribes of Arabs long before the days of Mohammed. Mohammed's tribe, the Quraish, adopted Allah as their primary tribal deity long before Mohammed was born.

Was it the angel Gabriel who supposedly spoke to Mohammed in the cave? I want to protest it was not the angel Gabriel. The God of Abraham, Isaac, and Jacob was not behind that revelation.

The Bible makes it perfectly clear that anyone who does not trust in Jesus as their Savior is not going to heaven, no matter how many times they pray every day or how sincere and pure-hearted they are. It is a mistake for us to believe that Muslims are such good people that they no longer have to be evangelized. We must assert their rights to religious freedom under our Constitution but at the same time desire to share with them the Good News of Jesus Christ. The bottom line is, one billion Muslins are deceived.

Deception is a spiritual force that every Christian has to deal with in life. First Timothy 4:1-2 says, "Now the Spirit expressly says that in latter times some will depart from the faith, giving heed to deceiving spirits and doctrines of demons, speaking lies and hypocrisy, having their own conscience seared with a hot iron."

I know of Christian leaders in America who were raised in a conservative evangelical background. They were taught that Jesus is the only way to heaven, but today they are preaching an inclusive gospel. In essence, they are saying that Jesus is not the only way to heaven and that there will be Hindus, Buddhists, Muslims, and others in heaven who have never heard of Jesus.

To those who posit such a message, I ask the question, "Why did Jesus have to die then?" There's no reason for the Son of God to give His life and to suffer the unspeakable horrors of Calvary if mankind can find its way to God some other way.

There is something devilishly clever about deception. When you're tempted you know it, when you're accused you know it. But when you're deceived, you don't know it. Let me warn you, beware of deception. James 1:22 declares, "But be doers of the Word, and not hearers only, deceiving yourselves." When we hear God's Word and don't practice it, we open ourselves to self-deception. This is the beginning of the path downward. Galatians 6:3 says, "For if anyone thinks himself to be something, when he is nothing, he deceives himself." How easy it is to take credit for our accomplishments rather then give honor to God's grace in our lives.

Four verses later in verse 7 Paul says, "Do not be deceived, God is not mocked; for whatever a man sows, that he will also reap." This is an irrevocable law of God. Deception is thinking that you can somehow escape His law. But you won't.

Here's a powerful verse in James 1:26, "If anyone among you thinks he is religious, and does not bridle his tongue but deceives his own heart, this one's religion is useless." Gossip is one of the most common faults of the body of Christ. Deception is thinking it doesn't matter what you say about people. I don't want my religion to be useless, so I do my best to bridle my tongue.

Deception operates in many forms. Look at this verse again in 1 Timothy 4:1: "Now the Spirit expressly says that in latter times some will depart from the faith, giving heed to deceiving spirits and doctrines of demons." It is a deceiving spirit that suggests that there are many ways to heaven. Some would argue for an inclusive gospel. It is inclusive. "For God so loved the world"— Muslims, Buddhists, Hindu's, everyone. But here's the catch: "That whosoever believeth in Him should not perish, but have everlasting life" (John 3:16 KJV.) They are all called upon to believe Him—that is, to believe on the name of Jesus.

People who believe the inclusive gospel have forgotten the primary teaching of the book of Acts. As you read the book of Acts, you cannot help but be overwhelmed at the incredible importance that was attached to the person and the name of Jesus in the early church.

"Through Faith in His Name"

In Acts 3 Peter and John had gone to the temple at the hour of prayer (three o'clock in the afternoon). This was the time of the day when the priest went into the holy place in the temple to offer the evening sacrifice to the Lord.

On this day there was a lame man lying at the gate of the temple. He begged for money from Peter and John as they came in. Peter looked at the lame man with eyes of faith and said to him, "Look on us" (v. 4 KJV), and the lame man thought that they had something to give him.

Peter's reply was so direct: "Silver and gold have I none; but such as I have give I thee" (v. 6 KJV). Peter had something to give the man that he didn't expect. Then Peter said, "In the name of Jesus Christ of Nazareth rise up and walk."

Notice Peter said, "Such as I have give I thee." Peter knew that God had given him something powerful, and Peter gave the man what he had. What he had was the name of Jesus.

As soon as Peter spoke, he took the lame man by the right hand and lifted him up, and his legs were healed. The man leaped and walked and praised God, running into the temple.

When the people saw this, they gathered by the thousands, wondering what had happened. Then Peter stood up to preach. The first thing he said to the people was, "Why look ye so earnestly on us, as though by our own power or holiness we had made this man to walk?" (v. 12 KJV).

Over the years I have discovered that oftentimes when God demonstrates His healing power, people believe it is the personal holiness of the messenger evangelist that has done it. Peter sensed this attitude among the people and corrected it immediately.

Their obvious question was, "How did you heal this man?" In verse 16 Peter stated the answer very clearly:

"And his name [that is, the name of Jesus] through faith in his name hath made this man strong, whom ye see and know. Yea, the faith which is by him hath given him this perfect soundness in the presence of you all."

What healed the man? It was faith in the name of Jesus. Peter wanted to address any deception that might have existed in that crowd, especially from the high priests. He addressed the error immediately with the truth concerning the name of Jesus.

Let me ask you a question: As you read these words, do you truly understand the power invested in the name of Jesus?

In Acts 4 Peter and John were called to account by Annas and Caiaphas, the high priests, and were asked a question, "By what power or by what name have you done this?" (v. 7).

Someone must have told the high priests about the use of Jesus' name. They were confounded. How could Peter and John bring healing to this man through using the name of someone they had just killed?

Then Peter, filled with the Holy Spirit, said to them directly, "Be it known unto you all, and to all the people of Israel, that by the name of Jesus Christ of Nazareth, whom ye crucified, whom God raised from the dead, even by him doth this man stand before you whole" (Acts 4:10 KJV).

There could be no question in anyone's mind that the healing took place through the power of the name of Jesus. In his mini-sermon to the high priests, Peter declared in Acts 4:12 KJV, "Neither is there salvation in any other: for there is none other name under heaven given among men, whereby we must be saved." Not Buddha, not Mohammed, not Confucius.

I would like you to meditate on that fact for a moment. Can you see the incredible awe and respect that Peter had for the name? Do we see that kind of respect for the name of Jesus in our churches today?

There's no question that the name meant something very special to the early church. They knew that Jesus had delegated to them His name, which gave them the power of attorney (covered in the next chapter) to use His name—and they did it. They went about healing the sick. They went about casting out demons. They went about raising the dead—all in the power of His name.

I find the reaction of the high priests very interesting. They wanted to be politically correct. They realized that the people knew that a remarkable healing had been done to the man. They decided to threaten Peter and John privately "that they speak henceforth to no man in this name."

They obviously realized the power was in the name. Their only hope of nipping this thing in the bud was to forbid them to speak in the name of Jesus. Acts 4:18 KJV says, "They called them, and commanded them not to speak at all nor teach in the name of Jesus."

Peter and John, when they were released by the Sanhedrin, went back to the believers. They gathered together for a mighty prayer meeting. Their prayer is recorded in Acts 4:29-30 KJV: "Lord...grant unto thy servants, that with all boldness they may speak thy word, by stretching forth thine hand to heal; and that signs and wonders may be done by the name of thy holy child Jesus."

Look at those words again, "that signs and wonders may be done by the name of thy holy child Jesus." The name of Jesus is a very powerful weapon that God has given to the church. When we use His name to heal the sick, when we use His name to declare the power of the Gospel, deception is destroyed at its root.

More Than a Signature

In Acts 5, revival spread throughout Jerusalem. The high priests were greatly troubled by what was happening, and they sent soldiers to bring in Peter and John for further questioning. They said, "Did we not straightly command you that ye should not teach in this name? And, behold, ye have filled Jerusalem with your doctrine, and intend to bring this man's blood upon us" (v. 28 KJV).

The early church didn't need a television advertisement to tell the people of Jerusalem what God was doing. The announcement came from the lips of the religious leaders of their day.

What doctrine did the early church preach? They literally had filled the city of Jerusalem with the doctrine of the name of Jesus. His name is much more than a signature to our prayers. The name of Jesus is the way a human being moves from the kingdom of darkness to the kingdom of light. The name of Jesus causes demons to tremble and sickness to flee. The name of Jesus is what empowered the early church. May God give us a revelation of the power of this weapon.

The high priests had the apostles beaten and again commanded them that they should not speak in the name of Jesus. They were trying to stop the doctrine that was filling the city; they were trying to stop the power of God that was snatching souls from their dead religion, giving them the life of the Holy Spirit, healing the sick, and bringing revival.

Then the apostles "departed from the presence of the council, rejoicing that they were counted worthy to suffer shame for his name" (Acts 5:41 KJV). Notice those words, "they rejoiced that they were counted worthy to suffer shame for his name."

They were suffering for the name. They were suffering for the use of the name. They were suffering for the authority of God that had been delegated to them through the name, and consequently they were beaten because that name had such great power on their lips.

As the story continues in Acts 8, revival begins to spread beyond the confines of the city of Jerusalem. Philip the evangelist preached in Samaria, and there God gave him a mighty revival. Verse 12 states, "But when they believed Philip preaching the things concerning the kingdom of God, and the name of Jesus Christ, they were baptized, both men and women" (KJV). Philip preached two things: the things concerning the kingdom, and the name of Jesus Christ. I believe the marvelous miracles—the demon oppressed being set free, the sick and lame healed—were a direct result of that message.

When the believers scattered from Jerusalem because of persecution, they carried one thing with them— the power of the name. Everywhere they went, the name of Jesus went with them, and revival followed as a natural result.

In Acts, chapter 9, after Saul was confronted by Jesus on the Damascus Road, the Lord spoke to Ananias and told him to go to Saul, saying, "For he is a chosen vessel unto me, *to bear my name* before the Gentiles, and kings, and the children of Israel: For I will show him how great things he must suffer for my name's sake" (Acts 9:15- 16).

God told Ananias what Paul's ministry would be. He said that the focus of Paul's ministry would be to preach Jesus' name, and that he would have to suffer many things for that name.

In verse 21 of the same chapter, when Paul preaches after his conversion in the synagogue at Damascus, "The people were amazed, and said; Is not this he that destroyed them who called on this name in Jerusalem?" (v. 21).

The people knew that this was the same name that had caused the incredible consternation in Jerusalem. Now here is Paul in Damascus, preaching and using this same name and the authority of the name.

I hope the message is clear. What did Peter preach? The name of Jesus. What did Philip preach? The name of Jesus. What did Paul preach? The name of Jesus. This was not a single, one-time occurrence. It happened all through their ministries.

After a close examination of the book of Acts, it is impossible to get away from the conclusion that the early church was consumed with the power of the name of Jesus. They took it with them everywhere they went. They used that name, and when they used that name, signs and wonders followed. We can also see why those who wrote the New Testament continually exhort all believers in all generations to believe in and abide in the name of Jesus, which keeps us from deceiving ourselves and deceiving others.

CHAPTER 5

Tap Into Divine Power, Part 2—
The Name of Jesus

Christianity is the most politically incorrect religion in the world because it says there's only one way to God and that is Jesus Christ. Jesus is the way, the truth, and the life. He is the only Mediator between God and man.

When I travel throughout the Islamic world, I sense heavy deception like a blanket covering the minds of the people. They are blinded and cannot see the truth. But when I declare the name of Jesus as the Son of God, it pierces that deceptive blanket like a sword.

Let me return to the story of Haji that I began in the last chapter, and you'll see this to be true. Remember, I held my breath after telling Haji that his god and my God were not the same. Then I pointed out clearly that Jesus is the Son of God.

I had in my possession a beautiful little 16-page booklet our ministry has developed called *The Story of Jesus*. It tells Jesus' story from His birth in Bethlehem. It talks about the miracles, the parables, the Crucifixion, Jesus' resurrection from the dead, and His second coming. The last three pages of the booklet are the plan of salvation, so simple that a child can understand.

I handed Haji a copy of the booklet and invited him to read it. Immediately he stopped the car out in the desert and asked one of the men in the back to drive while he read.

He spent the next several hours immersed in reading that little booklet over and over again, finding truth and reality in the gospel. That's the power of our message. The power of our message is in the name of Jesus.

That is one reason why I'm doing everything I can to distribute *The Story of Jesus* booklet. Over 27 million copies have been printed in over 70 languages. I am told that for every booklet we place on the field, 10 people will read it. That's 270 million people who have been reached by *The Story of Jesus*. That is about 5 percent of the current population of the world. God's Word will not return void, and I know that many have been born again because they read that booklet.

I believe in the power of the name of Jesus. We have committed ourselves to telling the story of the power of His name around the world. Just think for a moment. *The Story of Jesus* can go where a preacher cannot go. It travels economically, has no passport or visa problems. It leaps language barriers and is never influenced by radical prejudice. It sails the oceans, treks the deserts, and trudges the jungle footpaths of every continent on earth. It knows no fear and flinches before no man. It takes no notice of scoffs, jeers, or insults. It never tires, but works twenty-four hours a day, even while we sleep. It is never discouraged, but tells its story over and over again. It will deliver the same message to rich and poor, king and commoner. It speaks without a foreign accent. It is more permanent than the human voice. It never compromises and never changes its message.

I have never seen *The Story of Jesus* tossed aside, but I've seen people fight over copies when there were not enough for everyone.

Recently my oldest son, Scot, and daughter-in-law, Kathy, flew to the rooftop of the world, Katmandu, Nepal. They were checking out a rumor that had come to us concerning *The Story of Jesus*. Here is Scot and Kathy's account of what happened:

From Katmandu, we flew north into the Himalaya Mountains, up almost to the border of Tibet. We were flying without instruments. You had to see the runway before you landed. The runway was cut out of the side of a mountain at 11,000 feet. We descended rapidly, banked left with the G-forces pressing us firmly against our seats and landed in less than fifteen seconds on the front wheel.

Our left wing tip was eight feet from the rock face, and on the right we looked down thousands of feet. There was no room for error.

We were greeted by a team of horsemen. We had to travel by horseback one and a half hours farther into the mountains. We had come to meet Chimi, the man who translated *The Story of Jesus* into the Lhoba language. The Lhobas are an unreached people group who live in the autonomous kingdom of Mustang near the border of Tibet. The kingdom still has a king, queen, and prince, who rule in tribal matters.

The majority of people that inhabit Mustang are Tibetan Buddhists. Three years ago the king invited a Christian from Nepal named Ramesh to stay as his guest for a few days. It is customary to bring a gift to the king, so Ramesh decided to give him *The Story of Jesus,* newly translated into the Lhoba's language.

The only person who had been qualified to do the translating of *The Story of Jesus* was in jail. His name was Chimi. He was a Tibetan Buddhist, serving a seven-year sentence for drunkenness and vandalism. He agreed to translate the book.

One day in prison, after several weeks of translating, he came to the part on the Crucifixion. He read it over and over and felt profoundly guilty and had to stop translating. After stopping and starting several times, he yielded to the conviction of the Holy Spirit in his heart and decided that he had to serve this "Son of God"—he had come to believe in the power of Jesus' name.

The moment he yielded his heart to Jesus, Chimi said he felt totally different. He was released from prison shortly after finishing the translation.

What is truly amazing is the fact that Chimi was the first known Christian among the Lhoba people, a tribe of 45,000. Ramesh took the new translation of *The Story of Jesus* [World Compassion paid for the printing of 5,000 copies] and went to see the king. He presented the new Lhoba translation to the king and queen. He became nervous when he heard nothing back from them the first night. But, the next day, the prince came to Ramesh and was deeply moved. He asked if he could personally distribute the rest of the booklets to their people.

Scot and Kathy also met another Lhoba on their trip named Kamal. Ramesh had given him *The Story of Jesus* in Lhoba two years before. At that time he had been cheating on his wife and drinking heavily. He said nothing about the booklet. However, several months later, when Ramesh visited his home, Kamal's wife took him aside and said, "What did you do to my husband? He has stopped drinking and visiting other women and is talking about this Man named Jesus all the time."

Ramesh realized what *The Story of Jesus* had done in Kamal's life. Since then Kamal has led twenty-five other Lhobas to the Lord. This story could be repeated a thousand times over from cities and villages around the world. The longer I live, the more I am impressed with the power of Jesus' name. That power comes through in His simple story.

Delegated Authority

You may be asking, "What does all this information have to do with me?" The Bible says in Matthew 28:18-19, "And Jesus came and spoke unto them, saying, All power is given unto me in heaven and in earth. Go ye therefore, and teach all nations."

Mark records a parallel account in 16:15,17-18, "Go ye into all the world, and preach the gospel to every creature. And these signs shall follow them that believe; In my name, they shall cast out devils; they shall speak with new tongues...they shall lay hands on the sick, and they shall recover."

It is interesting to notice that in Matthew 28, Jesus declared that all authority or power was given to Him. He then delegated that authority to the disciples and beyond them to every believer. In Mark 16 He says, "These signs shall follow them that believe in My name." If we believe in the name of Jesus, we will cast out devils, we will speak with new tongues, we will lay hands on the sick, and they shall recover.

Jesus has granted to the church the power of attorney concerning His name. In other words, we have been delegated to take the authority of the name of Jesus to the world. When God delegates something to us, we are made responsible for it.

The name of Jesus has been given to the church, and the church therefore becomes responsible for the use of that name. If we do not use the name of Jesus with faith, nothing happens. However, if we do use it with an awareness that His name is representative of the power of God, then we will see some of the same miracles the early church witnessed.

Power of Attorney

Some years ago I was scheduled to travel to Europe. I was also in the process of purchasing a new automobile. It was impossible to sign the documents before I left because the deal had not been finalized. I was told by a friend of something called "the power of attorney."

I went to a bank with one of the men in my office to sign a document that would give him authority to buy the car for me while I was gone. I signed my name at the bottom of the paper, and that gave him power to negotiate on my behalf. He could put his name on the contract for the new automobile, and it would be as good as my own.

As Jesus was on His way to heaven, He said to the disciples, "I am going to leave something with you. It's called My power of attorney. I am not going to be around, but the Holy Spirit will be here. I am going to send the *Parakletos*—our intercessor, consoler, advocate, and comforter.[1] He is going to remind you of something very important, the power of using My name."

After Jesus declared that all power in heaven and earth had been given to Him, He delegated that power directly to you and me. He commissioned us and granted us the power of attorney to use His name against the enemy.

When you use the name of Jesus, it's just as though Jesus were saying the words Himself. He assumes responsibility. When you use the name of Jesus with the authority that is given to the believer, it is as though Jesus Himself were doing the praying. You are calling forth into the situation the power of Jesus.

I am reminded of a story that I heard my father tell thirty-five years ago when I was a boy. The story came from Charles Spurgeon, the great English preacher. He had told the story first from his pulpit in London.

A woman had been hired by a very rich man to take care of his household. She served the rich man faithfully for over twenty years. When the rich man was about to die, he called the poor woman to his bedside and thanked her for her faithfulness to him. He had no heirs and decided to be generous to her. He wrote something on a piece of paper and handed it to her. She was grateful for this act of remembrance on his part because she lived in a little hovel on the outskirts of the city of London. She took the piece of paper home and pinned it up on the wall.

Many years later she became sick, and Spurgeon, the great preacher, was called to visit her. After he prayed for her, he walked around the room and noticed this piece of paper on the wall. He turned to the woman and asked her about it. She told him the story. He asked her, "Can you read?"

She said, "No, I've never been taught how to read."

And then he said, "Madam, this piece of paper is a check for a great deal of money. You did not have to be living in these poor circumstances. You could have been living in the finest houses in London, eating the finest food."

How true this is for many of us concerning the name of Jesus. The Word of God tells us we have been granted the power of attorney to use that name. It is like a blank check that God has written and signed, and yet we have never cashed it in. We have never taken the name and done with it what God intended to be done with it. When we cash the check, signed in the name of Jesus, that check will be honored by God in the banks of heaven. The devil has to answer and respond to the power of the name of Jesus.

Some years ago I was invited to conduct a meeting on praise and worship with Christian artist Don Moen on the West Coast of the United States. We saw a powerful manifestation of the healing power of God in our services. On the opening Sunday morning of the meeting, a man stood up and requested prayer for the pastor. He said, "Every time I get on my knees to pray, I feel that the pastor is in great danger. There's going to be an attack made on his life." We prayed in response to the man's request, and I put it out of my mind.

Two days later in the meeting, we had a tremendous time of healing and deliverance. When the main service was over, I continued praying with needy people in the back room for about two hours. Later, as I left the service, I walked back through the sanctuary of the church. A woman was sitting in the dimly lit building. As I walked by her she reached out and grabbed my sleeve. She said, "You must pray for me now."

I was very tired. I did not feel that I had the strength to pray for her. I encouraged her to come back the next night, but she insisted. As I looked into her eyes, I was aware of the fact that she was being tormented. I realized immediately where the source of the torment came from, and I decided to minister to the woman.

I spoke to her and informed her that I was going to cast out an evil spirit that was oppressing her. When I addressed the evil spirit, I was very surprised. It did not speak in the woman's voice, but rather in a male voice. The spirit informed me that it was going to murder the pastor.

I had never encountered anything quite like this before. I informed the evil spirit that it was not going to murder the pastor, but it was going to leave the woman. I commanded the spirit to come out in the name of Jesus. As soon as I said "the name of Jesus," the woman began to tremble. The spirit began to shake the woman with real force. Finally, after a short time, the spirit left the woman, and she was free.

I did not discover until sometime later that she had been sitting in the sanctuary with a loaded 22-caliber pistol in her purse. She was waiting for an opportunity to shoot the pastor. She would have shot him within the next five minutes. The Spirit of the Lord led me to her at the right time, and the deliverance of God was there for her.

Many years later I met that same pastor in one of my meetings in a church in Colorado. He reminded me of that event and that night. He said, "Thank you for saving my life."

My reply was immediate. "I didn't save your life," I said. "It was the power in the name of Jesus that saved your life."

As I close this chapter, let me remind you again of the words of Jesus in Matthew, chapter 28, verse 18: "All authority has been given to me...Go ye therefore." Do you understand what happened when Jesus said those words? He was saying, "I have been given authority over Satan. This authority is Mine, and I have the right to give you power of attorney. I am transmitting My authority to the body of Christ. Your authority is in My name." I pray that the church will rise up once more and use the power of His name.

In Ephesians 1:17, Paul prays for the church that "the Father of glory may give to [them] a spirit of wisdom, and revelation, in the knowledge of Him, the eyes of [their] understanding being enlightened; that [they] may know...."

That is my prayer for everyone who reads these words. We need to spend some time meditating on the power that God has placed in the name of Jesus. It must get down on the inside of us, into our spirits, not just into our minds. We can't understand this intellectually. We understand it spiritually. And when you know the power of Jesus' name spiritually, you will realize the tremendous weapon that God has given to you to defeat and guard your heart and mind from all deception.

CHAPTER 6

No Longer Guilty, Part 1— The Blood of Jesus

One of the great old hymns of the church is entitled, *There Is Power in the Blood*. It says, "Would you be free from your burden of sin? There's power in the blood, power in the blood."[1]

Many of us over the years have been taught to believe that there is power in the blood of Jesus. But it's one thing to sing that song in church; it's another thing to know how to get the blood of Jesus to your address, in your life day by day.

Do you know how to activate the power of the blood of Jesus? In Revelation 12:11, Scripture says believers overcame Satan by the blood of the Lamb and the word of their testimony. Notice the relationship of those two things—the blood of the Lamb and the word of their testimony.

In this chapter I will show you how to use the blood as a powerful weapon against the accusation and guilt of the enemy. But first I want to look at the term "the blood of Jesus." What is meant by that?

Do you know where your blood comes from? How is blood created? Some years ago someone gave me insight concerning biology, and I learned some amazing things. I was told that there is no blood in male sperm or in a female egg. They do not have blood in themselves, but when the sperm and the egg come together at the time of conception, blood is created. It is created at the same moment that the new life begins within the womb.

In a natural birth, blood cells in the child come from both parents. At the moment of conception, the blood type of the child is determined immediately. It may be the blood type of the mother or the father. During the time of pregnancy, the baby is fed by the mother's blood, but it never comes in direct contact with the mother's blood. Why is this important? If the baby has a different blood type than the mother, the mother's blood would kill the child immediately. The baby is protected from this by the placenta, which keeps any flow of the mother's blood from the fetus.

It is important to know that although the blood of the mother brings food to the child, God has built a filtering system into the womb that removes the food from the mother's blood and then feeds it to the child. Therefore, the child never touches the mother's blood and there is no danger.

Why am I establishing this fact concerning blood? It is necessary for us to understand this process to understand the birth of Jesus. As the spotless, pure, and holy Son of God, Jesus could not carry contamination of His mother's bloodline. His blood had to be pure and undefiled. Jesus couldn't carry the stain of Joseph's bloodline either. Neither Mary nor Joseph's bloodlines could touch Him.

In some mysterious way that the Bible does not explain, the Holy Spirit overshadowed Mary. In Luke 1:35 the angel said, "The Holy Spirit will come upon you. The power of the highest will overshadow you. Therefore, also that Holy One who is to be born will be called the Son of God."

The blood type of Jesus could not be the blood type of His mother because of the miracle of His virgin birth. The blood type of Jesus came from the heavenly Father. When we talk about Jesus and His blood, we are talking about the blood of God.

"Life for Life"

I want to pursue this thought more fully in the Old Testament. In Leviticus 17:11 the Bible says, "For the life of the flesh is in the blood. And I have given it to you upon the altar to make atonement for your souls. For it is the blood that makes atonement for the soul."

Notice that phrase "the life of the flesh is in the blood." This is a very important biblical principle. This explains why the Bible declares in Exodus 21:23-24, "But if any harm follows, then you shall give life for life, eye for eye, tooth for tooth, hand for hand, foot for foot."

The principle is relatively simple. If something was destroyed, something of equal value must be given to replace it. Notice the use of the phrase "life for life." The words for *life* in New Testament Greek and Old Testament Hebrew are interesting words. There are three different kinds of *life* mentioned in New Testament Greek, and they are symbolized by different words: *psuche* refers to soul life, *zoe* speaks of eternal life, and *bios* speaks of natural life.[2]

In the Old Testament Hebrew, there is one primary word that speaks of the soul or life of a person, and that is the Hebrew word *nefesh*.[3] "And the Lord God formed man of the dust of the ground, and breathed into his nostrils the breath of life; and man became a living being," or a living soul (Gen. 2:7). The word for "living being" or "soul" there is the word *nefesh*. This really is a very dramatic verse.

Jehovah created Adam out of the dust of the ground, and then leaned over and breathed into his nostrils the breath of life. By this act He created a living being or soul. The Spirit of God breathed into the physical dust of man's body and created a soul. Adam became a person, a new life, a new personality—*nefesh.*

When Moses speaks of giving a life for a life, the Hebrew is *nefesh* for *nefesh,* or soul for soul. In the Old Testament if you killed someone in a criminal fashion, you would pay for the crime with the penalty of your own life.

Deuteronomy 19, verse 21 says, "Your eye shall not pity: life shall be for life, eye for eye, tooth for tooth, hand for hand, foot for foot." Again, the principle is the same—life shall be for life. That is *nefesh* in place of *nefesh.*

Later on in Leviticus 17:11 when God says to Moses, "The life of the flesh is in the blood," He is declaring the soul of the flesh is in the blood, or the personhood of the man is in the blood.

What does this mean? The Bible is clear in telling us that man is a tri-partite being. He possesses a spirit, a soul, and a body. The spirit by its very meaning has to do with our breath. When a man's spirit leaves his body (at the time of death), he ceases to breathe.

The soul of the man has to do with his blood. When a man's heart stops, the soul leaves the body. His blood flows no longer. Let me repeat, the Bible says the soul or the life of the flesh is in the blood. And God says powerfully in Leviticus 17:11, "I have given [this soul or life] to you upon the altar to make atonement for your souls." This is a divine principle, *nefesh* for *nefesh,* soul for soul, life for life.

In the divine concept of the atonement, one soul sheds its blood for another soul. Why is that necessary? Because the life is in the blood. Blood must be shed in atonement. It is the giving of one life for another.

In Isaiah 53:12, the prophet declares, "Because he poured out his soul unto death...." Other translations use the word *life*. Jesus poured out His life unto death. The Hebrew word is significant. It is the word *nefesh*.[4]

Here's what I want you to see. How did Jesus pour out His soul unto death? It was through His blood. His life was in His blood. When His blood was shed, His soul was given on behalf of all humanity.

In the movie *The Passion of the Christ,* I was overwhelmed to watch the death of Jesus on the cross. The movie graphically portrays how the soldiers whipped His back, how they pressed a crown of thorns into His head. They drove the nails into His hands and His feet. Even after He was dead, the soldier found it necessary to thrust a spear into His side, and out came water and blood. (See John 19:34.) The graphic portrayal of the shedding of His blood proclaimed the fact that He was offering up His soul on behalf of every man who would ever live—a soul for a soul.

I began this chapter with a biological examination of the blood of Jesus. I concluded that the blood of Jesus was the blood of God. I believe that God's life is infinitely more valuable than the sum total of all the life of His creation on this earth.

When the blood of Jesus was shed, it is the blood of God, the life or soul of Jesus being given on our behalf. God certainly overpaid for our redemption. The blood of Jesus was more than enough to atone for the sins of the entire human race.

Psalm 130:7 says, "With him is abundant redemption." How true that is! God paid a price that was worth far more than what I am worth. It was through the principle that God had established in Leviticus 17, a soul for a soul, a life for a life, that God redeemed the entire human race with the blood of His Son.

Frankly, I am disturbed at a trend that I see happening in many mainline denominations in America. For reasons that I don't understand, many people have begun to say that the blood of Jesus is not important. They are taking the songs about the blood out of their hymnbooks. This is dangerous because our eternal life in God was purchased by His blood and His blood alone. There is no redemption without the shed blood of Jesus Christ.

For this reason I want to strongly emphasize the fact that the life or the soul, the *nefesh*, is in the blood. Your spiritual life is a gift to you from God that comes only through Jesus' blood. His life streams into your life when the blood of Jesus cleanses you from all unrighteousness, makes you a new creation, joins you to Him as His child, and transforms you into the image of His Son. Thus the blood is vital to your faith and should always be remembered. There is power in the blood!

Operate in Abundant Life

Let me remind you that all of heaven watched the blood of Jesus being shed on the cross. They understand the importance of His life's blood. But believers must grow in the understanding of the power of the blood of Jesus. Even His first followers had trouble with this concept.

In John 6:54 Jesus shared a thought that horrified some of His disciples. Because He spoke this, the Bible says that many of them followed Him no longer. (See v. 66.) Jesus said, "Whoever eats My flesh and drinks My blood has eternal life, and I will raise him up at the last day."

To the average human being, that idea sounds offensive. There's something about blood that makes one's stomach turn over. Why did Jesus say these words? Because the life of God is in the blood. For us to have the life of God, we must drink the blood of Jesus. When do we do that? We do that by faith in salvation. We do that in the taking of the Lord's Supper.

Here is a principle that needs to be emphasized. The only Person in the universe who has life within Himself is God. Because we are God's creatures, we all receive our life from Him. That is what the word *nefesh* means. It speaks of a life that is dependent on another source, life that does not initiate itself.

When Adam became a living soul, he did so when God breathed into the dust, which was his physical body. The life in Adam depended on the breath of God. The concept is clear—Jesus gives life; life is found in the blood of Jesus; there is power in the blood; and that power is the very life of God.

One of my favorite Scriptures is John 10:10. "I have come that they may have life, and that they may have it more abundantly." Where do we get our spiritual life? All of us are dependent upon God for that life. And the only channel of eternal life that God has provided is the blood of Jesus.

If we want God's life, we must recognize that it comes to us through the blood of Jesus. When your faith understands this and appropriates the power of the blood of Jesus, you will automatically operate in more abundant life. Can I say that again? The more you understand the power of the blood of Jesus in your life, the more God's life will be activated in your life.

What a powerful truth is released when we look at the cross. The cross was the means that God used to release His life into our domain of earth. God's life had only been in heaven, but then His life was transmitted by a divine act of the Holy Spirit into the womb of Mary. When the blood of Jesus was shed on the cross, the life of God was released to everyone who would believe in that blood. The blood of Jesus contains the actual life of God, and God has chosen the channel of the blood of Jesus to bring life to you and me.

Can I say it again? I love that wonderful hymn that says, "There is power, power, wonder-working power, in the precious blood of the Lamb."

Satan, the Accuser of the Brethren

In Revelation 12:11 the Bible says, "And they [believers] overcame him by the blood of the Lamb and by the word of their testimony, and they did not love their lives to the death." This verse tells us that the powerful blood of Jesus overcomes the accusations of the devil.

In the previous verse, John the Revelator declares, "For the accuser of our brethren, who accused [believers] before our God day and night, has been cast down." There's no question that Satan is the accuser of the brethren. I've already dealt with that fact earlier in this book.

In this section, I want to examine how Satan becomes the accuser of the brethren, and then finally how the blood deals with Satan's accusation.

All of us are troubled by recurring guilt problems of one kind or another. Sin-consciousness has held many Christians in bondage for years. Whenever anyone preaches against sin, they say, "That's me." They are constantly aware of the effects of sin in their life. They've never really come into a revelation concerning the realities of the new creation.

Man has a highly developed sin-consciousness, a spiritual inferiority complex, a sense of unworthiness that dominates him. The church has been very strong to denounce sin in the life of the believer and has lacked in presenting the truth of what we are in Christ Jesus by faith.

We hear condemnation preached from the pulpit, rather than the declaration of our righteousness in Christ Jesus. Guilt is one of the most powerful psychological forces in a human being.

Satan, as a master strategist, knows how to manipulate us because of our guilt feelings. As a young man wanting to serve God, there were many times I almost gave up because I had no way of dealing with the overwhelming guilt when I did sin. Satan knew me better than I knew myself. He knew how to trigger within me a sense of sin-consciousness that constantly robbed me of spiritual victory. After I repented, I still felt guilty.

My father used to tell a story many years ago that carries a tremendous message. A minister had a friend who was a caretaker in a zoo. One day they imported a new snake from the continent of Africa. The zoo keeper invited the minister to come and watch a strange phenomenon. He took a little sparrow, opened the door of the snake cage, and threw the sparrow in.

When the little bird saw the snake, it was terrified. It fluttered around in the farthest corner away from the snake. The snake did not chase the bird. He simply lay coiled in the corner and fastened his beady eyes upon the bird.

The little bird gradually stopped its fluttering, and the minister realized it was slowly being hypnotized by the eyes of the snake. Soon the little bird hopped down off its perch. The snake opened its mouth, and the little bird jumped in.

Paul talked about the tremendous power of sin. He called it the "mystery of iniquity." (See 2 Thess. 2:7.) There is something hypnotic about sin and guilt. If your eyes are fastened on your weaknesses, you will try as hard as you will, but you will not be able to break the power. Why? Because you are hypnotized by the power of the thing you're trying to stop.

We are always looking inside ourselves for the willpower to say no to the sins that plague us. This is the believer's struggle with living under the Law or living under God's grace. *Law* drives us to perform so that we will be accepted by God. *Grace* is being accepted by God, and in our intimate relationship with Him we appropriate His grace to do right. Without understanding grace, we are always trying to please God but never feeling accepted, constantly moving but never arriving.

Have you ever seen a guinea pig on a treadmill? My grandson Taylor has a little guinea pig. It lives most of its life in a cage. When it wants to exercise, it gets on a treadmill and runs as fast as its little legs will carry it. It runs fast, but it doesn't go anywhere. It stands in the same spot, while the wheel revolves faster and faster.

I see many Christians like that little guinea pig. They are on a spiritual treadmill. They come under the preaching of the gospel. They are convicted of their sin and guilt. They confess to the Lord, sometimes with strong crying, "Lord, forgive me this one time, and I promise You I will never do it again."

They go along for a certain amount of time, perhaps two weeks, a month, then two months. Everything seems fine. Then they are caught on their blind side. They trip up and fall, committing the same sin again, and they feel so worthless.

They come back to God and say, "Lord, forgive me just one more time." But even as they pray, there's a certain sense of hopelessness and helplessness inside. They have tried so many times by sheer willpower, and yet they continue to fail.

First John 3:21 KJV says, "If our heart condemn us not, then have we confidence toward God." When you experience guilt continually in your life, you cannot operate in strong faith toward God. Guilt makes us miserable because we feel unworthy of God's love, protection, and provision. So we don't want to pray. We can't believe Him for healing. We can't believe Him for answers to our financial problems. When we want to praise Him, we do it halfheartedly or not at all. There's a voice inside us that says, "You're a hypocrite. God won't hear you." And so we go around and around, sinning, feeling guilty, repenting, but allowing Satan's cloud of condemnation and shame to remain. So what happens? We have no grace from God to stand against the sin, we continue to feel guilty, and we end up doing it all over again—we are on the sin treadmill.

One of Satan's weapons against humanity is guilt. He can easily use this weapon on believers because most Christians do not know how to discern between guilt and Holy Spirit conviction. They assume that their incessant guilt feelings — even after repentance — come from the Holy Spirit when they are actually coming from the unholy spirit (the devil).

"Not Guilty"

The Bible says in John 16:8, the Holy Spirit "convicts the world of sin, and of righteousness, and of judgment." Notice the three things that the Holy Spirit addresses: sin, righteousness, and judgment. These are different from guilt. The Holy Spirit does not use guilt. He says, "You did this. It's wrong. You need to repent and put it right."

This is how you do that. Once you have confessed and repented and done whatever is necessary to make restitution, the matter is closed. You don't think about it again. There's nothing more that you can do. You must learn to leave it alone.

Ephesians 1:7 says, "In him [Christ] we have redemption through his blood, the forgiveness of sins according to the riches of his grace." The term "the forgiveness of sins" in this verse proceeds directly from the blood of Jesus. The word *forgiveness* here is translated remission in other versions. When God remits your sin, He wipes out all memory of it. It involves the complete removal of the transgression or offense.

When the blood of Jesus is applied to your sin, God doesn't know that you did it. There's no record in heaven of your past. God has applied His bulk eraser. Your sin has been forgiven and remitted. The Holy Spirit will convict you. When you repent and trust the blood of Jesus to remit your sin, the issue is taken care of.

It is the devil who continues to bring up your mistakes. It is the devil who continues to remind you of your past. He is rightfully called in Scripture "the accuser of the brethren." This is the problem that guilt generates. You never know if you've done enough to please God and "make up for" your wrongdoing.

You may know someone you have hurt or offended. You've tried to make it right. You've repented for it, but somehow it doesn't matter. No matter what you say or do to the offended person, it is not enough. It is never enough. That is not conviction from the Holy Spirit. That is the power of guilt operating through the accusations of Satan.

Someone needs to put up a sign for believers that says, "Believer beware. Guilt is a denial of the work of the Cross." Again, it is very different than the specific conviction of the Holy Spirit. Guilt never ends. It is oppressive. It goes on and on. But when conviction comes from the Holy Spirit, we deal with our sin and that settles it. We get back up and walk on with the Lord, free from the weight of sin and guilt.

If you are dealing with issues that never go away, if nothing you do is ever sufficient, you are dealing with guilt. I suggest that you stand on various Scriptures in the Word. Isaiah 54:17 is one: "'No weapon formed against you shall prosper, and every tongue which rises against you in judgment you shall condemn. This is the heritage [or inheritance] of the servants of the Lord, and their righteousness is from Me,' says the Lord."

This verse is such good news that it's more than enough to shout about. No weapon the devil devises against you shall prosper. Be cool. Relax. He will try to revisit the subject of your past sins over and over again, but he will ultimately fail if you are standing on the blood of Jesus.

When you read the above verse carefully, notice it says, "every tongue which rises against you in judgment, *you shall condemn.*" Underline *you*. It doesn't say that God will condemn. It says that you must condemn. You do that by understanding the power of the blood. You do that by telling the devil that your past is gone. Your sin is remitted. God can't see it anymore, and you won't look at it. You say, "Devil, shut up about it!"

Think of it for a moment, the devil is not challenging *your* righteousness. He is challenging the righteousness that God transferred to you through the blood of Jesus. When you condemn him for trying to put a "guilt trip" on you, you are using God's weapon of the blood of Jesus to stop him in his tracks by declaring you are the righteousness of God in Christ Jesus. You are saying to the enemy of your soul, "My life is the life of Jesus. His blood is my blood. And through His blood I am no longer guilty."

CHAPTER 7

No Longer Guilty, Part 2—
The Blood of Jesus

As we discovered in the last chapter, one of the keys to being free of unjust guilt and defeating the enemy's accusations is understanding our right standing with God through the blood of Jesus. We are righteous not because of our good behavior but because of Jesus' shed blood. We are righteous because we are in Him and He is in us. But there is more! Righteousness is also at the heart of the gospel.

Paul says in Romans 1:16-17 KJV, "For I am not ashamed of the gospel of Christ: for it is the power of God unto salvation to everyone that believeth; to the Jew first, and also to the Greek. For therein [in the gospel] is the righteousness of God revealed from faith to faith: as it is written, The just shall live by faith."

These two verses make one fundamental truth very clear. The gospel is given to us as a revelation of righteousness. The power of the gospel is that it declares a man to be righteous. If you have not understood your righteousness in the gospel, then you have not understood the heart of the gospel itself.

Many of us have been believing a half gospel for years. We have never been willing—or understood that we had the right—to take our stand in righteousness as the Word of God reveals it to us.

Let me ask you a question. Suppose a friend of yours is dying. You have five minutes to give him the gospel. What would you say to him? There are four points contained in the gospel, as revealed by Paul in 1 Corinthians 15:3-4.

For I delivered to you first of all that which I also received: that Christ died for our sins according to the Scriptures, and that He was buried, and that He rose again the third day according to the Scriptures.

The first point of the gospel is, *Christ died for our sins according to the Scriptures.* The second point is, *He was buried.* The third point is, *He arose again the third day according to the Scriptures.* The fourth point is, *we are made righteous when we believe these things.* That is where the power of the gospel is unleashed.

There's no power in being told that you're a sinner. The power is released when you believe that Jesus died for your sin, that He was buried, that God raised Jesus from the dead, and you are made 100 percent righteous when you believe these first three points. "For with the heart man believeth unto righteousness" (Rom. 10:10).

Paul said that the gospel is the power of God unto salvation. Why is it the power of God? Because in it the righteousness of God is revealed. That's the power point right there. The power is in the righteousness. The simple fact is that when you trust Christ, God makes you 100 percent righteous.

In 2 Corinthians 5:21 KJV Paul says it another way: "For he [God] hath made him [Christ] to be sin for us, who knew no sin; that we might be made the righteousness of God in him."

This verse describes a divine exchange. Jesus became our sin on the cross so that we could become His righteousness when we believe in Him. This solved the problem between God and mankind, which is that God is righteous and holy, but we are sinful.

How can a holy God fellowship with a sinful man? This is the challenge of redemption. Legally, God has to make us as righteous as He is Himself in order to have fellowship with us. Second Corinthians 5:21 explains it clearly. God made Jesus to be sin with our sin so that we might be made righteous with His righteousness.

It doesn't matter how you feel—guilty, depressed, isolated, or worthless—the fact remains that you are the righteousness of God in Christ Jesus. God has made you 100 percent righteous, no matter how you perform and no matter how you feel. There's no such thing as being 67 percent righteous. We are either 100 percent righteous, or we are not righteous at all. And you are as righteous as Jesus Christ is righteous.

Law drives you to perform so you can be righteous. *Grace* declares you are righteous, so now you are able to perform. There comes a time when you've got to start to turn from law to grace and say what God's Word says. "I am righteous."

This imputed righteousness means that every time God looks at you as His child, He doesn't see your own righteousness, which falls far short of His perfection. He sees you through the righteousness of Jesus. Therefore, you are as acceptable to God as Jesus is, regardless of your daily performance.

When did God make you righteous? He made you completely righteous the moment you placed your faith in Jesus as your Savior. God cannot add to that righteousness. He cannot improve upon it. And neither can you! You receive it strictly on the basis of faith alone. When you dare to believe this, when you dare to believe that God has made you completely righteous, you will walk away from your feelings of guilt and inferiority.

Let me say it clearly. The guilt and condemnation that is robbing you of faith comes from Satan. God declares that you are righteous through the blood of Jesus. The life of God in the power of Jesus' blood has eradicated your sin. There's no record of it, so forget about it because God already has forgotten it.

In Isaiah 43:25 KJV the Word says, "I, even I, am he that blotted out thy transgressions for mine own sake, and will not remember thy sins." Hebrews 8:12 KJV says, "For I will be merciful to their unrighteousness, and their sins and their iniquities will I remember no more."

If you've asked God to forgive you, He doesn't remember that you ever did anything wrong. When you believe that, you will be walking in the power of the blood of Jesus, the righteousness of God in Christ Jesus, no longer guilty.

Educate Your Heart

Romans 10:10 KJV says, "For with the heart man believeth unto righteousness." You must believe in righteousness with your heart. The devil will tell you that you are a liar. He will use all of the psychological guilt mechanisms from your past. He will tell you that you are rotten to the core, that God is going to judge you for your sin, that you are not good enough to serve the Lord.

Notice the second part of Romans 10:10 KJV, "For with the heart man believeth unto righteousness, *and with the mouth confession is made unto salvation.*" If you don't feel that the righteousness in your heart is real, then declare with your mouth the righteousness of God. Your heart will begin to believe what your mouth says.

That's how we educate our hearts. We educate our hearts with the words of our mouth. The English term "to learn by heart" essentially means to "learn by mouth." How did you learn the multiplication tables? You learned them by saying them over and over with your mouth until you knew them "by heart."

How do you know that you're righteous in your heart? You say it with your mouth over and over until your heart believes what your mouth is saying. What is your mouth saying? Your mouth is simply saying what the Word of God says. God's Word says you're righteous. But you've got to declare that with your mouth.

If we continue to confess our righteousness with our lips, God will open our spiritual eyes to the revelation of this powerful truth. We will begin to see ourselves being the righteousness of God in Christ. Then Satan will lose his ground of accusation. The devil is defeated when the believer understands what his righteousness means.

Notice Romans 5:9: "Much more then, having now been justified [made righteous] by His blood, we shall be saved from wrath through Him." This verse declares very clearly that you are made righteous by the blood of Jesus. Your righteousness is real because there's power in the blood of Jesus.

Let me remind you again of the verses in Revelation 12:10-11 KJV.

And I heard a loud voice saying in heaven, Now is come salvation, and strength, and the kingdom of our God, and the power of his Christ: for the accuser of our brethren is cast down, which accused them before our God day and night.

And they overcame him by the blood of the Lamb, and by the word of their testimony; and they loved not their lives unto the death.

Notice the Scripture declares very simply that believers overcame the devil by the blood of the Lamb and the word of their testimony. There is power in the blood of Jesus. But you and I must testify to this fact. That's how we overcome the accusations of the enemy.

This verse tells us to testify to what the blood of Jesus does for us. The blood of the Lamb overcomes Satan and his accusation. Let me say it again. We must testify daily to what the blood of Jesus does for us. When we do this, Satan's accusation is defeated in our lives.

What Happened to the Blood?

You may be saying in your heart, "I believe there's power in the blood of Jesus, but where is His blood today, right now? He died two thousand years ago. What happened to His blood?"

Hebrews 9:12 KJV gives us an answer.

Neither by the blood of goats and calves, but by his own blood he entered in once into the holy place, having obtained eternal redemption for us.

After Jesus died and rose from the dead, this verse indicates that He went into heaven with His blood to obtain eternal redemption for us. He brought His own blood into the holy of holies before God in heaven. He placed His blood on the altar before God. That blood is there on that altar today, as freshly slain as it was two thousand years ago when Jesus Christ died on the cross. Jesus entered into the "Holy of Holies" with His blood. It is that blood that makes you righteous.

You may be thinking, *I must deal with guilt and accusation every day of my life. I need the blood applied to my address on a regular basis. How do I do that?* In Exodus 12 we have a beautiful analogy of how to make the blood work in our lives. Israel had been in bondage to Pharaoh for four hundred years. Moses had gone to Pharaoh, commanding him to let God's people go.

Pharaoh refused, and God through Moses performed ten plagues that came on the land of Egypt. The tenth plague was the worst. The death angel moved through the land, and every house that was not covered by the blood of an innocent lamb was smitten. That meant that the oldest boy-child in the home was slain by the death angel.

God designed a plan to protect the children of Israel. He told them the head of every household should slay a lamb, collect the blood of the lamb in a basin, and then sprinkle the blood on the two side posts of the door and the lintel over the top of the door. Then the house and all its inhabitants would be safe.

The challenge for the leader of the household was to get the blood onto the doorpost. God instructed them to take a weed-like herb called hyssop and dip it into the blood, which was contained in a basin. Then, with the hyssop, the blood was sprinkled onto the doorpost.

Our testimony concerning the blood of Jesus is like the hyssop used in the Old Testament by the children of Israel. When they dipped the hyssop in the blood and sprinkled it on the doorpost, that is a picture of us giving testimony to the power of the blood of Jesus.

Our testimony takes what the Word says about the blood and applies it to the doorposts of our lives on a daily basis. When we declare to the devil that we are made righteous by the blood of Jesus, we are living and walking in the power of the blood, which is the righteousness of God in our lives.

The enemy of your soul and mine knows that when you discover this, you will not be afraid of him any longer. He knows that your days of guilt and inferiority are over. The accuser cannot accuse when the ground for accusation is taken away. The blood takes your sin away. The blood has erased your past. There is no ground for accusation.

Here is the key. When you get your eyes off of the snake—the sin that so easily besets you—and get your eyes focused on the power of the blood—the fact that the blood has eradicated the sin, the fact that the blood has made you righteous—you will be victorious.

Don't be hypnotized by the snake any longer. Don't focus on your weakness and try to stop sinning by your own willpower. Turn your eyes from the weakness and temptation to the blood of Jesus that has made you righteous. Appropriate the grace of God to say no to sin and temptation. Then glorify God with your lips, declaring the power of the blood. Live in fullness of joy because the blood of Jesus makes you righteous. And when guilt, condemnation, and shame attack your mind, overcome the accuser by the blood of the Lamb and the word of your testimony.

What Does the Blood Do for Us?

There are so many things the blood does for you. According to Ephesians 1:7, it redeems you and remits and eradicates all your sin. According to 1 John 1:7, the blood of Jesus continually cleanses you from all sin.

According to Romans 5:9, by the blood of Jesus you are made righteous. According to Hebrews 13:12, the blood of Jesus sanctifies you and makes you holy. According to 1 Corinthians 6:19-20, the blood of Jesus makes your body the temple of the Holy Spirit. According to 1 Peter 2:24, by His stripes [blood], you were healed.

There are so many things that are done for us by the blood of Jesus. *Included in the blood of Jesus is the power of God to protect us.* When the Old Testament Israelites sprinkled the blood of the lamb on the doorposts of their home, their homes were protected from the evil one.

Personally, I believe that when I speak the power of the blood in my life, my life is especially protected from the work of the evil one. Let me illustrate what I'm saying.

Protected by the Blood

One month after the tragedy of 9-11, I sensed the Lord speaking to my heart about getting involved in this war-torn country of Afghanistan. We endeavored to help widows and orphans inside of the borders of Afghanistan, and we used the city of Quetta, Pakistan, as the base of our operation.

One day we were asked to take nine truckloads of food and humanitarian goods into an Afghan refugee camp called Mohammed Khail. There were 90,000 Afghan refugees who lived in this camp on the flat desert, situated on the border between Afghanistan and Pakistan.

I sent the nine truckloads of humanitarian aid into the camp early one morning. An hour after they arrived, I arrived with my eldest son, Scot, and my associate, Joel. As I got out of the Jeep, I realized that some of the refugees were looting our trucks. But when I moved to stop them, I was met by a hail of rocks. They started to stone us!

Apparently there were leaders of the Taliban living in this camp. This fact was unknown to the leaders of the UN who oversaw and ran the camp. The Taliban stayed in the refugee camp at night and would go across the border into Afghanistan to fight each morning.

Without my permission or my knowing it, one of our aid workers had placed a huge sign on the side of one of the trucks that said, "World Compassion USA." That's why the people began to stone us. The people in the camp regarded America as the oppressor, and the sign advertised that we were Americans.

The refugees were determined to kill us. One of the stones hit my driver in the nose. When I looked at him, blood was running down onto his shirt. Then a huge rock took out the windshield of one of our trucks. I put up my hands to protect my face and yelled to one of the drivers, "Is there anywhere safe in this place?"

He said the United Nations had a headquarters about three miles through the refugee tents and mud huts. So I said, "Head for it. It's the only place of safety around here."

Our nine trucks and three Jeeps began to rumble through the refugee camp on our way to the UN headquarters. By this time, there were probably three thousand people chasing us and throwing rocks. Six windshields and windows were destroyed on that trip.

The UN headquarters was surrounded by a nine-foot-tall green fence with huge doors. It was a large enclosure. We were able to get all of our trucks and Jeeps inside. As we pulled into the compound and the gates slammed behind us, it reminded me of the wild West days in America.

The provincial authorities in Pakistan had sent six armed soldiers with us, so I assumed that we were safe. But no sooner had the doors slammed behind us when suddenly hundreds of the enraged mob started coming over the walls. They wanted to kill us. I could see it clearly in their eyes.

Just after pulling into the fort, a huge rock came through the car window beside where Joel sat. His first thought was that it might be a grenade, but it wasn't. Nevertheless, the soldier sitting beside me, who had an AK47 in his hands, was shaking. He opened the back door of the Jeep, stood up, and began to fire his machine gun into the air. The effect was magical. The gunfire scared the people off the wall, but they kept throwing rocks over the wall and broke more of our windows.

When I got out of the car, one of the local people in the fort began to jump up and down beside me, saying, "What do you think? You're going to die today. You're going to die today."

I said, "No, I'm not going to die."

But he insisted, "Yes, you are. These people are going to kill you. You'll never get out of here alive."

"No," I said, "I'm not going to die today. I'm protected by the blood of Jesus." Of course, that man did not know what I was talking about. He may have thought I was crazy, but I really didn't care. I knew that even as the blood protected the houses of the children of Israel from the power of the death angel, God would keep me from death by the power of the blood.

Within half an hour ten thousand people had gathered around the outside of the fort, sitting on their haunches in their long, flowing garments. Their dark eyes were filled with anger, and they were holding large rocks in their hands. They sat and stared at the fort. They had moved about a hundred yards away from the wall, wary of the range of the soldiers' guns.

The first thing we did was to unload all of the humanitarian aid we were carrying. There were 44-pound bags of flour, cooking oil, tea, sugar, cooking utensils, blankets and jackets to protect them from the bitterly cold nights of the desert.

After two hours and the unloading of our trucks, we decided to make a run for it. They threw open the gates, and our lead truck lurched toward the crowd but stopped after about five seconds, when a huge rock took out his windshield. He backed up into the fort, and we slammed the gates shut again.

It was only after all means of escape seemed exhausted that we remembered our satellite phone. Just before we had embarked on this trip, I had asked Scot to purchase one. The director of the UN camp had a phone number for a military base a few miles away from the refugee camp, so we used the satellite phone to call the base for help.

The military base immediately dispatched soldiers with Jeeps, machine guns, and trucks. And four hours after all this began, they rolled up to the fort. After negotiating with the leaders of the crowd, we were told that it was time to go.

I will never forget sitting in the back seat of the Jeep as we drove through the doors of the fort. The people from the refugee camp were still sitting on their haunches with rocks in their hands. I noticed that the hands of the Pakistani soldier sitting beside me with an AK47 were still shaking. But because of the large military force, the crowd didn't move to stop us. We got out of the camp and onto the highway. We were free!

A week after we were gone, a pastor from the area came back to the fort, gave out the food to the people, preached a gospel message from the Scriptures, handed out *The Story of Jesus* booklets, and explained the plan of salvation. So the mission was successful in the end.

Some days later, there was a great uproar in the Pakistani government when they discovered that the provincial authorities had allowed us into the camp without giving us adequate protection. You may say, "Don't things like that scare you? Isn't that dangerous? Weren't you almost killed?"

Yes, but we were also protected by the blood of Jesus. We overcame Satan by the blood of the Lamb and by the word of our testimony. When you do the same thing, not only will you be protected, but you will defeat any attempt of Satan or his demons to make you feel guilty. As you declare with your mouth what the blood does for you, you will release the power of the blood of Jesus into your life.

CHAPTER 8

Your Mouth Is the Launching Pad

Every one of God's weapons have to be launched through the human mouth. When Jesus used the sword of the Spirit, which is the Word of God, against the devil in the wilderness, He said, "It is written." When Peter healed the lame man at the gate of the temple, he commanded healing in the name of Jesus through the vehicle of his mouth.

We overcome the accusations of the devil by the blood of the Lamb and by the word of our testimony. The mouth is the key to so much in the Christian life. I believe the mouth is the key to victory in warfare.

Your mouth can speak healing or sickness, blessing or cursing. Matthew 12:37 KJV says, "For by thy words thou shalt justified, and...condemned." Proverbs 10:11 KJV says, "The mouth of a righteous man is a well of life." Proverbs 12:14 says, "A man shall be satisfied with good by the fruit of his mouth." Our words are like seeds that are sown in the ground. They will produce after their kind, and we will reap the harvest of our words.

In this chapter I want to look at the power of the mouth. First, we will examine the power of God's mouth. Then, we will look at the power in our mouths. And finally, we will look at the power in Jesus' mouth.

God's Words

In examining the creative power in God's mouth, we need to understand one fundamental guiding principle that is established in the Scripture. It is this: God's Word and God's Spirit should always work together in perfect unity and harmony. We should never divorce the Word from the Spirit or the Spirit from the Word. It is not God's plan that the Word should ever work in opposition to the Spirit or that the Spirit should contradict the Word. They always agree.

This principle is illustrated in one of the psalms of David that we looked at earlier. Psalm 33:6 says, "By the word of the Lord the heavens were made, and all the hosts of them by the breath of his mouth." When you examine the verse carefully, the Bible is declaring that the heavens and all the hosts of them were made by two things: the word of the Lord and the breath of His mouth.

Remember, the Hebrew word for "breath" in this verse can actually be translated as "Spirit." So you could translate the verse, "all the hosts of heaven were created by the word of the Lord and by the *Spirit* of His mouth." Here we have a beautiful picture of God's Word and God's Spirit working together. As God's Word goes out of His mouth, His Spirit—which is His breath—goes with it.

It is impossible for a human being to speak words without using breath in the pronunciation of the words. When you say the word "people," you expel breath as your lips pronounce the word. It is actually impossible to speak an entire sentence without using your breath at the same time. It is necessary for breath to go forth with our speech.

God has created us in His image. He speaks the same way. When God speaks His Word out of His mouth, His breath goes with the announcement of the Word. Remember, the breath is His Spirit. So you see, when God speaks, the Spirit goes out of His mouth with His Word and gives the Word power.

In Genesis 1:2 the Bible says, "The Spirit of God was hovering over the face of the waters." In verse 3 we read, "Then God said, 'Let there be light.'" Notice the presence of two things: the Spirit of God and the Word of God announcing the creation of light. Here you have the Word and the Spirit working together. Creation of light took place when God spoke the words, "Let there be light." The Spirit went forth as He said those words, and light came into being. This principle is one of the great principles of faith that believers need to understand.

When God's Word and His Spirit come together in our mouths, we speak with the actual creative authority and power of God Himself. If we try to divorce the two, we will get off the road into a ditch. If we seek only to see the manifestations of the Spirit without lining them up with the Word, we will fall into deception, fanaticism, and error. If we hold only to the Word without the anointing of the Spirit, we will end up in powerless orthodoxy and religious tradition.

Photographic Image

I would like to illustrate the power of God's mouth by looking at the creation of man in the Old Testament. In Genesis 1:26 KJV the Bible says, "And God said, Let us make man in our image, after our likeness: and let them have dominion over the fish of the sea, and over the fowl of the air, and over the cattle, and over all the earth, and over every creeping thing that creepeth upon the earth."

Notice the two phrases, "Let us make man in our image," and "after our likeness." The word "image" is very interesting in the original Hebrew. It is the word *tselem*.[1] In Bible commentaries it is referred to as "shadow."[2] This word, however, is used in the modern Hebrew language, and it means to have your photograph taken.

The Word is giving us a powerful picture of man being made in the image of God. We are a photograph of what God looks like. In other words, man has been made after God's outward physical outline and form.

Did you know God has a physical form, and in our outward appearance we project the likeness and image of God? There are constant references in the Scriptures to the fact that God has hair, eyes, a nose, and feet. The Bible tells us that Jesus is at the right hand of the throne of God. (Mark 16:19.) He's not at the left hand.

People often misrepresent God because they have no knowledge of Him through Scripture. In the Bible, He is not some vague form or mysterious glory cloud. He does have outward physical form. And this verse tells us that mankind is made in His image. That's why Jesus was incarnated as a man. He too bore the image of God the Father. (See Heb. 1:3.)

When you realize you are made in the outward image of God, it affects the way you think about yourself. The image that you see in the mirror when you get up in the morning is formed after the image of Almighty God. No wonder the Bible says we are fearfully and wonderfully made. (See Ps. 139:14.)

Genesis 1:26 also points out that we are made after God's likeness. The Hebrew word used here indicates an inward comparison, an inward likeness.[3] Even as God is a triune God made up of three persons—God the Father, God the Son, and God the Holy Spirit—

mankind is also a triune being. Man is spirit, soul, and body. (See 1 Thess. 5:23.)

To understand this, it is best for us to go directly to the verse that describes God creating Adam in Genesis 2:7. This verse gives a description of the actual process of creation, the record of man being born the first time. (Later on, I would like to compare man being born again the second time.)

The *King James Version* of this verse says, "And the Lord God formed man of the dust of the ground, and breathed into his nostrils the breath of life; and man became a living soul." There are several interesting facts about this verse. The first one is the use of the term "Lord God" in the text. This is the first time this word for God appears in the Old Testament.

In Genesis 1 God is referred to as *Elohim.*[4] It is a plural word that implies God is a trinity—Father, Son, and Holy Spirit. The word used for *Lord* in Genesis 2:7 ("Lord God") appears in the *King James Version* as *Jehovah.*[5] This word is composed of four consonants, y-h-w-h. The vowels in a word are not written in Hebrew, and no one knows what vowels should be put between these four consonants that refer to God.

Modern scholars use the word *Yahweh,* which means, "I am who I am." I believe there's a reason for its use. In John 1: 1-3 KJV it says, "In the beginning was the Word, and the Word was with God, and the Word was God. The same was in the beginning with God. All things were made by him; and without him was not any thing made that was made." Notice verse 3 of the text: "All things were made by him." Who does "him" refer to in this verse? It refers back to verse 1. "In the beginning was the Word."

The Word in this text refers to Jesus Christ, the Son of God. And the declaration here is very simple. Jesus Christ, the Son of God, made all things. Notice the latter part of verse 3: "without him was not any thing made that was made." The entire Godhead was involved in creation. God the Father designed the plan. Jesus Himself was the agent of creation. And the Holy Spirit brought forth creation by His power.

Notice that Jesus was actively involved in creating all things. This perhaps will shed new light on Genesis 2:7 for you. I believe that Jesus is directly involved in creating Adam in this verse. The Word, the eternal Word, is active here. Jesus as the Word of God is in the process of creating the first man. I believe that is why the term *Jehovah,* speaking of God in His personal sense, is used in this context. In this reference, Jehovah refers directly to Jesus Christ.

Back to Genesis 2:7: "And the Lord God formed man of the dust of the ground." The word "formed" is the Hebrew word *yatsar,* and it means to mold into a form.[6] It carries the idea of a potter forming clay. It also has within it a reference to something that is done with great attention to detail and precision.

In the creative process, God did everything well, but it seems that when it came to creating man He took special care when He formed man out of the dust of the ground. In other words, His attention is especially focused upon the creation of Adam. The Scripture says man was formed from the dust of the ground. There obviously must have been some kind of moisture in that dust to make it adhere and take shape.

I think a better word to use in this text would be *clay.* Can you see the picture here? It is so powerful if your faith can grasp it. Jesus molds a body of clay on the ground. It is an absolutely perfect sculpture, better than anything man has ever tried to design or make on his own. I see a picture in my mind's eye of that sculpture, that body of clay lying on its back, a lifeless form.

Then the verse says, "The Lord breathed into his nostrils the breath of life." Can you see Jesus (the Word) kneeling beside the form of Adam on the ground? God stoops down to breathe life into the clay. What a dramatic picture this is! God the Son (Jesus) stooping over the clay and putting His nostrils to the nostrils of the about-to-be Adam, placing His lips on the lips of Adam. And then He breathes the divine breath, the breath of God, into that lifeless form. The Spirit of God enters the clay, and the clay becomes a living person. Notice God's Word coming forth from God's mouth.

What incredible power we see manifested here! Adam comes alive with real hair, real eyes, the ability to hear, an incredible nervous system. His heart begins to beat. The blood courses through the veins and arteries. The glands function. The tissues are perfectly formed. The hands, the fingers move—all created by the power of God's breath.

This is God's Word going forth out of God's mouth.

Just a sidebar to this picture: If God created us so perfectly the first time, then He can heal us just as easily when something goes wrong with the original creation.

Back to Genesis 2:7. The latter part of the verse says, "And man became a living soul." I would like to point out that in this verse you have man in three parts: spirit, soul, and body. All three parts are referred to in the verse. When God breathed His breath into man, man came alive spiritually as well as physically.

You have within you the eternal breath of God. You have a spirit. But notice God breathed into the dust or the clay of the ground. It was the clay that became the body. Notice also that the union of the breath of God and the molded clay brought into being a third part that is called the soul, and man became a living soul. That word in Hebrew is the word *nefesh*.[7]

So there you have it—spirit, soul, and body. The soul was created when the Spirit came in contact with the body, and in that sense the soul remains as the point of contact between your spirit and your body.

Breath of Life

Perhaps the best way to understand the mystery of creation is to look at the very expressive Hebrew words that are used for spirit and soul. One of the Hebrew words for *spirit* or *breath* is *ruach*.[8] The last two letters, c-h, have a sound that doesn't exist in English. I heard it first on one of my missionary journeys to South Africa in the Afrikaanse language. You will also hear it in the accents of the Scottish people. We call it a soft aspirated h or c-h. When a Scotsman says *Loch,* he pronounces the c-h with a semi-guttural sound. All Semitic languages have this sound. In order to pronounce it, you have to produce a continuing outgoing breath. When a Scotsman says *loch,* he can continue on with the c-h as long as he has breath.

Remember, we are talking about the power of the Spirit of God coming out of God's mouth. The Spirit of God is represented by God's breath. The Spirit is the continuing outgoing breath of God. The word *ruach* represents that breath of God to us. It is the Spirit coming out of God's mouth who initiates all life. Because He is life,

He breathes life out to all of mankind. This is what happens when God's Word and His Spirit are combined.

We just saw that one of the words for *soul* in the Hebrew is the word *nefesh*.[9] Remember, I mentioned that in Hebrew you don't write the vowels. So in writing this word in Hebrew, you would write four different consonants, n-f and s-h. In pronouncing these consonants, you have a sound that is very similar to sleeping. You inhale or breathe in with the pronunciation of the n, and then you expel with the pronunciation of the f and the s-h. It sounds like a person in a deep sleep. If you say the word to yourself, you will immediately hear what I'm referring to.

Notice the order, however. First you breathe in, and then you breathe out. This is a true depiction of the human soul. The soul is dependent life. It must first breathe in the breath of God. That's what Adam did. He breathed in the breath of God. And then the human being breathes out its own soulish life. The soul must receive before it can give out. The spirit originates and gives. The soul receives and then gives.

To sum up, we see Jesus kneeling over the form of Adam. He places nostril to nostril, lips to lips, and then in the power of the Holy Spirit He breathes into the man. It is a very powerful outgoing breath. It carries with it the explosion of divine energy. This is the life of God. And Adam comes alive. What a powerful picture of the first birth!

What does the Bible means when it talks about the second birth? What did Jesus mean when He said to Nicodemus, "You must be born again" (John 3:7)? In John 20 we have an interesting story about the resurrection of Jesus. In the evening time on the day of resurrection, the disciples had gathered together because they were afraid of the Jews.

Suddenly, Jesus stood in the midst of them and said, "Peace be unto you" (v. 21 KJV). He showed them His hands and His feet, and the Bible says the disciples were glad when they saw the Lord.

Then Jesus said to them, "As my Father hath sent me, even so send I you." Notice specifically verse 22 KJV: "And when he had said this, he breathed on them, and saith unto them, Receive ye the Holy Ghost."

Notice, He breathed on them. And as He breathed on them, He spoke the Word of God. He said, "Receive ye the Holy Ghost," or receive divine breath. This picture brings us back to the story of the first creation as we see Jesus bending over Adam and breathing into him the breath of God's life.

In John 20 Jesus, the eternal Word, breathes on His disciples and says, "Receive ye the Holy Ghost." Here is Jesus through the energy of the life-giving Spirit, transmitting the very energy and nature of God into the spirits of the disciples. At that very moment, the disciples were born again. They experienced the life of God in their spirits. The miracle of the new birth took place. They were born again through the power of the living Word. When you understand this dramatic biblical picture, other Bible verses will take on new meaning for you.

In Isaiah 55:11 the Word says, "So shall My word be that goes forth from My mouth; It shall not return to Me void, but it shall accomplish what I please, and it shall prosper in the thing for which I sent it."

Here again is the picture of God's Word and His Spirit, or His mouth. "So shall My word be that goes forth from My mouth." The Word and the Spirit are working together here.

In Matthew 4:4 KJV the Bible says, "Man shall not live by bread alone, but by every word that proceedeth out of the mouth of God." Again, the Word is proceeding out of the mouth; the Word and the Spirit are working together with power.

This brings me back to the distinction I made earlier concerning the two words translated "the Word of God" in Scripture—the words *logos* and *rhema*. *Logos* is the unchanging self-existent Word of God. It is God's counsel settled in eternity before time began, due to continue on into eternity long after time has run its course. It is the entire Bible from Genesis to Revelation.

It is of this divine *logos* that David speaks in Psalm 119:89 KJV when he says, "For ever, O Lord, thy word is settled in heaven."

On the other hand, *rhema* is derived from a verb meaning "to speak" and denotes specifically a word that is spoken,[10] something that occurs in time and space.

In Romans 10:17 KJV Paul says, "Faith cometh by hearing, and hearing by the word of God." He uses the word *rhema,* not *logos* in this text. When we consider, "Faith cometh by hearing," we know that we can't hear something that has not been spoken. In order to be heard, a word must be spoken.

This is what happens when the Holy Spirit takes a part of the vast *logos* of God and speaks it to your heart under the anointing. The *rhema* spoken by the Holy Spirit becomes a living voice speaking to your heart. God Himself is speaking directly and personally to you.

Working Together

Apart from the Holy Spirit, there can be no *rhema*. In the Bible we have the total counsel of God, but it is too vast and too complex for me to comprehend in its totality. *Rhema* is the way the Holy Spirit brings a portion of *logos* down out of eternity and relates it to time and human experience. *Rhema* is that portion of the total *logos* that applies at a certain point in time to my particular situation.

The initiative is with God in *rhema*. God knows better than we do just what part of the Bible will meet our need at any given time. The Spirit directs us to the very words that are appropriate and then imparts life to them so that they become a *rhema,* a living voice. At that point, God expects you and me to hear. To the extent that we hear, we receive faith.

This is graphically illustrated in Isaiah 55, verses 8-13.

"For My thoughts are not your thoughts, nor are your ways My ways, says the Lord.

"For as the heavens are higher than the earth, so are My ways higher than your ways, and My thoughts than your thoughts.

"For as the rain comes down, and the snow from heaven, and do not return there, but water the earth, and make it bring forth and bud, that it may give seed to the sower and bread to the eater,

"So shall My word be that goes forth from My mouth; it shall not return to Me void, but it shall accomplish what I please, and it shall prosper in the thing for which I sent it."

Isaiah is talking about the heavenly plane and the earthly plane. God's ways and thoughts are in heaven. This is the divine *logos,* the Word of God forever settled in heaven. The earthly plane contains man with his ways and thoughts, far below those of God. But God has a way of getting His ways and thoughts brought down to man.

The picture is graphic. Like the rain and the snow that bring heaven's life-giving moisture down to earth, God says, "So shall My word be which goes forth from My mouth." Underline that phrase "goes forth from my mouth." This is the same *rhema* that Jesus speaks of in Matthew 4:4—the Word that proceeds out of the mouth of God.

This is the Word by which a man is to live. It is a portion of the heavenly *logos* coming down to earth as *rhema*. It is like the rain and the snow. It causes the earth to bear and to sprout. It gives "seed to the sower, and bread to the eater."

When you and I receive this *rhema* spoken to us out of the mouth of God, it brings forth fruit in our lives. It brings healing. It brings abundance. It brings the blessing of God.

In Matthew 4:4, Jesus answered Satan and said, "It is written, 'Man shall not live by bread alone, but by every word that proceeds from the mouth of God.'" Jesus declared that man should live by every *rhema* that proceeds directly from God's mouth. Notice, the verb "proceeds" is very important. It is in the ever-present tense in the Greek, which means it is proceeding all the time. There is a *rhema* word proceeding out of the mouth of God and coming to us on a daily basis. That *rhema* is to become our daily bread. It is always fresh. It is always *proceeding*.

Rhema is like each of the broken pieces of bread that Jesus fed to the multitude. It is suited to each need. Many times when *rhema* comes, it will come to us through another's hands. The key for us to see, however, is that in order for *logos* to become *rhema*, the Holy Spirit must speak the Word to us (in our heart). The Word and the Spirit work together.

The Power of Confession

We come now to the second part of this chapter, the power of man's mouth. In Romans 10:10 KJV the Bible says, "For with the heart man believeth unto righteousness; and with the mouth confession is made unto salvation." Notice that it is with the mouth that we confess our salvation.

A parallel Scripture is found in Mark 11:23: "For assuredly I say to you, "Whosoever says to this mountain, 'Be removed and be cast into the sea,' and does not doubt in his heart, but believes that those things he says will be done, he will have whatever he says."

Both of these verses illustrate the power of the human mouth. Mark 11:23 says we will have whatever we say. Romans 10:10 says, "With the mouth confession is made unto salvation." The word *unto* here in Greek indicates motion or progress.[11] In other words, we move progressively forward into the benefits of salvation as we continue to make the right confession with our mouth.

The Greek verb *sozo* in the New Testament is usually translated "to save." It contains the total idea of salvation, which goes far beyond the forgiveness of sins. It includes God meeting every one of our human needs.[12] The word *sozo* is used for the healing of the woman with an issue of blood. (See Matt. 9:21-22.) It is used for the healing of the cripple at Lystra, lame from his mother's womb. (See Acts 14:8-10.) It is used for the deliverance of the Gadarene demoniac from a legion of demons and his being restored to his right mind. (See Luke 8:36.)

The word *sozo* is used for the raising of the daughter of Jairus from the dead. (See Luke 8:49-55.) The prayer of faith that restores the sick to health in James 5:15 is also called *sozo* or salvation.

New Testament salvation includes deliverance, healing, and protection. It includes every benefit that God has for us—spiritual, physical, financial, material, temporal, or eternal. These blessings are all summed up in one, great, all-inclusive word—salvation.

The Scripture is very direct. It says that if you want to enter into the various benefits of salvation, how do you do it? With the mouth confession is made unto salvation. That is the key. The clear way to lay hold of every area of God's provision has to do with the confession of our mouth.

The word "confess" in this text comes from the Greek verb *homologeo*. Its translation means literally "to say the same thing as."[13] Thus, New Testament confession is saying what God is saying; our confession is always in agreement with God's Word. Therefore, New Testament confession is saying the same thing with our mouth as God says in His Word. It is making the words of our mouth agree with the written Word of God.

In 2 Corinthians 4:13 Paul says, "And since we have the same spirit of faith, according to what is written, 'I believed and therefore I spoke.' We also believe, and therefore speak." Speaking words from your mouth is the natural way for you to express your faith in God and His Word. Faith that does not speak dies in the heart.

In Matthew 12:34 Jesus says, "For out of the abundance of the heart the mouth speaks." Verse 37 says, "For by your words you will be justified [or made righteous], and by your words you will be condemned."

One of the great truths of Scripture is the emphasis on the fact that there is a direct connection between our mouth and our heart. They are connected and cannot be separated. And they affect one another.

The *New American Standard Bible* translates Matthew 12:34 as, "For the mouth speaks out of that which fills the heart." In other words, the mouth is the overflow valve of the heart. Whatever comes out through that overflow valve indicates the contents of the heart. If our heart is filled with faith, then our mouth will express faith. If we speak words of doubt and unbelief, they indicate that doubt and unbelief exist in our heart.

Romans 10:8-10 KJV declares:

> *"But what saith it? The word is nigh thee, even in thy mouth, and in thy heart: that is, the word of faith, which we preach;*
>
> *That if thou shalt confess with thy mouth the Lord Jesus, and shalt believe in thine heart that God hath raised him from the dead, thou shalt be saved.*
>
> *"For with the heart man believeth unto righteousness; and with the mouth confession is made unto salvation."*

Notice the words "mouth" and "heart" appear in all three verses. But also notice the order in which they appear. In verses 8 and 9, mouth appears first, then the heart. But in verse 10 the order is reversed. The heart comes first and then the mouth.

This is what happens in our practical experience. When we confess the Word, we make the words of our mouth agree with the written Word of God. As we do this, we receive it into our heart. The more persistently we confess God's Word with our mouth, the more firmly it becomes established in our heart.

After doing this over and over, faith becomes established in our heart and no conscious effort is needed any longer to make the right confession. Faith naturally flows out in what we say with our mouth because our heart is full of the Word.

As we continue to express our faith through our mouth, we confess our way progressively into all the full benefits of salvation. In the Hebrew language, the phrase "to learn by heart" could be "to learn by mouth."[14] That's the practical way in which we achieve the result. To learn things by heart, you say them over and over with your mouth until you know them by heart.

That is how we learned our multiplication tables. My most difficult tables were the sevens—seven times six is forty-two, seven times seven is forty-nine, seven eights are fifty-six, and so on. I used flash cards when I started, but after I had said the multiplication tables long enough, my heart captured what my mouth was saying. Eventually the flash cards were no longer needed because the tables were in my heart. Today, if someone asks me what seven times eight is, I don't need a calculator or flash cards. Out of my heart comes the answer.

This is why the Bible tells us to meditate and confess God's Word—so that we can think and speak like God. Whenever a need arises in your life or your faith is challenged, your mouth must declare what God's Word says about the situation. If sickness attacks your body, your mouth declares what the Bible says: Matthew 8:17, "Himself took our infirmities and bore our sicknesses"; 1 Peter 2:24, "By his stripes you were healed"; Isaiah 53:4, "Surely He has borne our griefs [sicknesses] and carried our sorrows [pains]."

Our feelings will probably prompt us to say something that does not agree with God's Word. Our challenge is to ignore our emotions and to continue to speak God's Word out of our mouths. We make the words of our mouths agree with God's Word. This is New Testament confession.

When Satan attacks your life, you need to find Scriptures that answer the satanic assault. Then you need to confess those Scriptures with your mouth in order to silence the accuser of the brethren. Romans 8:1 declares, "There is therefore now no condemnation for those who are in Christ Jesus." When the devil accuses you and points out your failures and the many times you've made mistakes, you must declare what God's Word says. Remember, you overcome Satan by the blood of the Lamb and the word of your testimony. (See Rev. 12:11.)

There will be times, especially in the confession of physical healing, that you will be caught in the tension between the symptoms of your physical body and the unchanging truths of God's Word. It is then that you must stand on God's Word. You must confess God's Word, just like you confessed the multiplication tables. No matter how bad the symptoms become, your spirit makes the right confession: "By His stripes or wounds I was healed."

If you're going through a time of financial shortage, remind yourself of 2 Corinthians 9:8: "And God is able to make all grace abound toward you, that you, always having all sufficiency in all things, may have an abundance for every good work." Dare to confess that God is making His grace abound to you, that you always will have all sufficiency in everything, that the revealed level of God's provision in your life is abundance. Then watch God confirm His Word in your life and in your financial situation.

Every problem that we encounter becomes a motivation to make the confession that declares God's answer to that problem. The more complete and consistent our confession, the more fully we enter into the experiential enjoyment of our salvation.

We now come to the third part of our chapter. We have discussed God's mouth and our mouth. Now we will take a look at Jesus' mouth.

A Guarantee of Fulfillment

The book of Hebrews is a wonderful book that speaks primarily about the high priesthood of Jesus Christ. As our High Priest, Jesus has gone in to sit on the right hand of our Father. As our High Priest, He ministers as our personal representative in the presence of the Father. He covers us with His righteousness. He offers up our prayers. He presents our needs personally to God. And as our High Priest, He becomes the guarantee for the fulfillment of God's promises on our behalf.

Many believers have never understood the true picture of what Jesus is doing on their behalf at the right hand of the Father. However, as you examine the book of Hebrews, you find out that the high priesthood of Jesus is directly connected to the words of your mouth. In other words, your confession affects what Jesus is able to present to the Father on your behalf.

To make it simple, the confession that we make on earth determines the extent to which Jesus is free to exercise His priestly ministry on our behalf in heaven. Hebrews 3:1 says, "Therefore, holy brethren, partakers of the heavenly calling, consider the Apostle and High Priest of our confession [or profession], Christ Jesus." Notice that Jesus is called the "High Priest of our *confession.*" This links His priesthood directly to what we say with our mouths.

Remember, the word *homologeo* or "confession" means "to say the same as." Confession takes place when we declare with our mouths what God says in His Word. Obviously Jesus is listening to the words that come out of our mouths; He is the High Priest of our confession. Each time we make the words of our mouths agree with God's Word, that makes His priestly ministry effective on our behalf.

I pray that the Holy Spirit will open your eyes to see how important the words of your mouth are. How many times do believers bring their complaints, their arguments, their backbiting to Jesus, but He can't take that to the Father because we are not declaring God's Word. If we fail to make the right confession, if we confess doubt or unbelief rather than faith, then Jesus cannot act as our High Priest.

When you make the words of your mouth agree with God's Word, you are guaranteed that your High Priest will offer those words to the Father on your behalf. Hebrews 4:14 declares, "Seeing then that we have a great High Priest who has passed through the heavens, Jesus the Son of God, let us hold fast our *confession*." Once again, the high priesthood of Jesus is connected directly to our confession. And we are counseled in this verse to hold fast to our confession.

Once we have declared God's Word with our mouths, if the circumstances don't line up soon, how easy it is to go back to confessing the negative. When the pressures rise, when the waves of the ocean begin to lash us with unbelief and defeat, we must hold fast to our confession, hold fast to what the Word of God says about our situation. Why? Because Jesus is bringing the words of our confession to the Father.

Finally, let's look at Hebrews, chapter 10, verses 21 and 23. "And having a High Priest over the house of God...Let us hold fast the confession of our hope without wavering, for he who promised is faithful." This is the third time in the same book that the writer connects the high priesthood of Jesus to the words of our mouths, or our confession.

In verse 23 he says, "Let us hold fast the confession of our hope without wavering." It seems that the writer anticipates the fact that when you take a stand on God's Word, the pressures are going to increase. The temptation to give up on God's Word will seem over-whelming. So in verse 23 he says to us, "Hold fast to the confession of your hope without wavering."

No matter how many pressures come against us, victory comes only when we hold fast. So don't waver. Don't give up! Why? Because your High Priest is bringing your confession directly to the Father. Your confession links you to a High Priest who will bring your petitions to the Father because you are praying His Word and His will. Then His Word can be done on earth as it is in heaven. If you hold fast to your confession, God will answer your prayer.

Speak Blessings Into Existence

Let me summarize what I've said in this chapter. The creative power of the universe is tied up with God's Word being spoken from God's mouth with the power of God's Spirit.

Remember, God said, "'Let there be light'; and there was light." God's Word comes to us on a daily basis through the revelation of the Holy Spirit. It is a *rhema* word: "Man shall not live by bread alone, but by every [*rhema*] that proceeds [every day] out of the mouth of God."

Like the rain and the snow, God's *rhema* comes down from heaven, and it comes to life in our hearts by the power of the Holy Spirit. When that *rhema* word becomes alive inside of us, we must speak it with our mouths. "With the mouth confession is made unto salvation." Every blessing that salvation provides, we speak into exis-tence by the power of God's Word in our mouth.

"Whoever says to this mountain, 'Be removed and be cast into the sea,' and does not doubt in his heart, but

believes that those things he says will be done, he will have whatever he says."

Mark 11:23

As our mouth continues to speak the Word of God, our High Priest in heaven takes note of our confession. The High Priest of our confession, Jesus Christ, brings those words of our mouth directly to the attention of God the Father.

The theme of this book has been how to conquer the thought attacks of the enemy, how to overcome the thoughts that Satan introduces to our minds. We have seen that God has given us three weapons: the Word, the Name of Jesus, and the blood Jesus shed on the cross at Calvary. Each of these weapons is activated by the words of your mouth.

Your High Priest in heaven is listening to what you say about the Word, the Name, and the Blood, and what you say determines what will happen in your life. Your confession determines the manifestation of your salvation because "With the mouth confession is made unto salvation." Always remember that your mouth is the launching pad for God's will and Word to be done in your life—and for the enemy's attacks against you to be utterly defeated.

CHAPTER 9

Hope: The Mind's Defense, Part 1

I never cease to be amazed at the powerful influence of our thoughts. In writing this book, I have been impressed all over again with how random thoughts are. I find myself thinking thoughts that seem to come from nowhere. We all have these random thoughts. How many times have you heard someone say, "I just had a thought out of the blue"?

In researching this subject, I've discovered that thoughts come from three places. First of all, they come to us through the five senses—sight, hearing, touch, taste, and smell. Probably 80 percent of our thoughts come to us from the natural stimuli around us. I believe the greatest single source of the world's pressure in our contemporary culture is television. I'm not saying that all television is wrong, but your television set brings the world into your home. Television entices and manipulates. It is a demonstration of spiritual control on a vast scale.

The aim of most television advertising is to make you want things you do not need and to buy things you cannot afford. It must be working because advertisers are spending billions of dollars trying to get their message across to you and me through our TV sets.

Television and media are prime vessels for the enemy to introduce ungodly thoughts and thinking patterns to our minds.

After the five senses, the second area from where thoughts come is the subconscious mind, or our memory. Every one of us has a reservoir of remembered experiences. Have you ever wondered how a memory can suddenly be triggered in your mind? It may be something that happened many years ago in your past, something you thought you had forgotten; but some kind of stimulus brings it back to your conscious mind in a vivid picture. Your subconscious is the second source of thought in your mind.

The third area from which thoughts proceed is the spiritual world. There are two sources of power in the spiritual world. One is God, and the other is the devil. One is good, one is bad. There's no question that God gives thoughts to His children. Every time you pick up your Bible and read it, you are reading a book of God's thoughts. There is incredible power in the thoughts of God, power that will heal you and bless you in every part of your life. But just as God speaks to us through His thoughts, so the devil comes to us with his thoughts.

The Word of God says that you can control your thoughts. *You* are responsible for doing something with your thoughts. Again, let me emphasize that the main power of Satan over us is through suggestion in our thought life.

Put On the Helmet of Hope

I have wondered over the years why there are so many people in the church who suffer from a spirit of depression, who are worried, full of fear, and speak nothing but pessimism and cynicism. Surely if the enemy has such freedom to attack us in our thought lives, God must have provided some sort of defense that would allow you and me to stop this satanic attack.

We have already seen that God has given us the offensive weapons to defeat all attacks of the enemy—the Word, the Name, and the Blood. I have outlined these for you. They put you on the offense instead of the defense. By the power of the words of your mouth, you release those weapons against temptation, deception, and accusation.

But I have discovered that God has also given us defensive armor to protect our mind from Satan's thoughts. I found this item of defensive armor in that well-known Scripture passage in Ephesians 6:13-17:

> *Therefore take up the whole armor of God, that you may be able to withstand in the evil day, and having done all, to stand.*
>
> *Stand therefore, having girded your waist with truth, having put on the breastplate of righteousness,*
>
> *and having shod your feet with the preparation of the gospel of peace;*
>
> *above all, taking the shield of faith with which you will be able to quench all the fiery darts of the wicked one.*
>
> *And take the helmet of salvation, and the sword of the Spirit, which is the word of God.*

Paul outlines six items of defensive armor in this portion of Scripture that will protect a believer against satanic attack. Please notice, however, that although God has provided all of this armor to protect you, it is your responsibility to put it on. Just because you are born again and have given your life to Christ does not mean that you automatically have any of this armor in place.

It is your responsibility as a mature Christian to take up the whole armor of God. You've got to gird your loins with truth. You have to put on the breastplate of righteousness. You have to see that your feet are shod with the preparation of the gospel of peace. You've got to take up the shield of faith. You've got to put on the helmet of salvation. This is a very dramatic truth. Please think on this for a moment. God has provided the defensive armor, and it is *His* armor. But you must put it on.

In these items of defensive armor provided here, there's only one piece of armor that protects the head or the thoughts—the helmet of salvation. In verse 17 Paul says, "And take the helmet of salvation." The helmet is like a hat. It covers your head.

I believe scripturally this is the one thing that will protect your mind and your thoughts. In preparing to write this book, I began to research the meaning of the helmet of salvation. That sounds very generic. What does a helmet of salvation mean? I found another Scripture that speaks of the helmet. In 1 Thessalonians 5:8 Paul says, "But let us who are of the day be sober, putting on [notice again, we must put it on] the breastplate of faith and love, and as a helmet the hope of salvation."

Paul says that we must put on the helmet of the hope of salvation. If you don't put on the helmet, then you are leaving your mind unprotected. Few Christians know how to control their thought lives. If you put on the helmet, it will help you. Again, let me point out, the helmet is called "the helmet of the *hope* of salvation." I believe there's something about hope that protects our mind and our thoughts.

There's a wonderful verse in 1 Corinthians 13:13 that most believers memorize in Sunday school. "And now abide faith, hope, and love, these three; but the greatest of these is love."

Paul is reminding us in this verse that there are three abiding spiritual realities in our life, three things that we must develop with all the spiritual energy that we can muster. We are to seek them. Why? Because they will abide forever. These three things will carry us through life and make us a success. What are the three things? Faith, hope, and love.

Let me ask you a personal question. How many sermons have you heard on faith over the years? I have heard hundreds of sermons on faith. How many sermons have you heard on love? Probably hundreds. When was the last time you ever heard a sermon on hope? I remember hearing one sermon on hope in the last thirty-five years. Hope is the forgotten message of the body of Christ.

I believe because we have forgotten to emphasize the importance of hope in the New Testament, we have left the minds of believers open to depression, worry, fear, pessimism, and cynicism. Essentially, our minds have been left unprotected. Why? Because we didn't understand how important hope was. Let me state again, I believe that hope is the forgotten message in the body of Christ.

Hope is not an option for you. It is the helmet that you must put on. It is impossible to please God without faith, and you must develop faith. God is love and you cannot please God without learning to love. But God is also a God of hope, and He expects us to do something about developing the principle of hope in our spiritual lives.

More Than a Positive Attitude

Let's get down to a definition of what hope is. There are two kinds of hope expressed in the New Testament. The first meaning in the New Testament is wishful thinking. In Romans 15:24, Paul says,

"Whenever I journey to Spain, I shall come to you. For I hope to see you on my journey and to be helped on my way there by you."

In this context, Paul says, "I hope to see you." In other words, "I am wishing that if everything works out, I will be with you at such and such a time." That is wishful thinking.

How often have you heard someone say, "I hope we have good weather next week"? Depending on where you live, that may be possible, or it may not be possible. We use hope in this sense in contemporary English. "I hope she does that. I hope he can see this." We are wishing for it. It is wishful thinking.

However, there's another definition for New Testament hope. This is the second meaning of hope, and it is a powerful word in the New Testament. The best definition that I have been able to discover for hope is *a confident expectation of the goodness of God.*

Let me counsel you to meditate on those words for a few moments. Repeat them over and over to yourself. When you dare to believe and have a confident expectation of God's goodness in your life, you are practicing New Testament hope.

Hopelessness is one of the saddest conditions in the human experience. I continually travel all over the world. I am in Muslim countries many times every year. Everywhere I go, I see hopelessness written on the faces of people. I see this in China among the atheist communists. I see it in India among the Hindus. You cannot sit in an airport very long and look at the faces of people without being impressed by the fact that much of the human race is hopeless. They have no hope.

A hopeless person is a weak person. Why are they weak? They have no backbone. Hopelessness takes away a person's backbone.

They have no motivation or inspiration. "Why should I do it? Why should I keep going? It's hopeless." They give up very easily. I have seen the blank stare of hopelessness in our world far too often.

Scripture tells us that there are three abiding realities: faith, hope, and love. We are to pursue all three of these in our spiritual journey. The church has been faithful to pursue faith and love but negligent to pursue hope. Then we wonder why our faith is not working and our love keeps dying. It is because we have neglected the hope of salvation. That means that God is on our side. We can expect His goodness, favor, and grace to flow into our lives.

I came down from my native Canada many years ago to attend Oral Roberts University in Tulsa, Oklahoma. I have heard Oral Roberts preach hundreds of times. He's one of my favorite preachers in the world. From the first time I heard him, he has always spoken the same sentence to open his messages. You can depend on him to address an audience with this statement: "Something *good* is going to happen to you."

Although I have heard him say this hundreds of times, I did not appreciate it until now. As a young student at the university, I thought, *This is a good positive mental attitude. This is a good way to get the audience ready to receive the Word of the Lord.* In my naiveté and spiritual immaturity, I did not understand the importance of his words.

When Oral Roberts declared, "Something *good* is going to happen to you," he was imparting to us one of the clearest and simplest explanations of New Testament hope that we will ever find. The essence of hope is that God has got something good for you now and in your future.

Hope is a confident expectation of God's goodness. When you or I say, "Something good is going to happen to me," we are making a public declaration of our New Testament hope in God. In 1 Thessalonians 1:3, Paul says, "Remembering without ceasing your work of faith, labor of love, and patience [steadfastness] of hope in our Lord Jesus Christ...." In this verse we again have all three qualities: faith, love, and hope.

Paul mentions the work of faith. How true that is. Faith must be expressed by works. Faith that doesn't act is dead. Then he speaks of a labor of love. Labor means real hard work. True love doesn't sit around and sympathize. It rolls up its sleeves and does something.

Then notice the steadfastness of your hope. There's something about hope that creates endurance, perseverance, and patience. You and I need hope that perseveres, that doesn't give up, that is in it for the long haul.

Expecting Good

One of the best verses in the Bible that defines hope for me is Romans 8:28: "And we know that all things work together for good to those who love God, to those who are the called according to his purpose." What a declaration Paul makes in this verse! God is working all things together for good. That is the perfect definition of New Testament hope.

There are two qualifications to God working all things for good in the verse. You must love God, and you must be called according to His purpose. If those two requirements are fulfilled in your life, you can be sure that God is causing everything to work together for good for you.

Ask yourself, "Do I really love God? Am I doing what God called me to do?"

God has a purpose for every person. Everything that comes to pass in your life is for the fulfillment of that purpose. If you're not walking in the purpose for which God has called you, then stop, repent, turn around, and get on the right track. If you do that, you are guaranteed that God is working all things together for your good.

This verse of Scripture does not allow pessimism at all. This Scripture gives you a foundation for total, never-failing optimism. You cannot read and believe Romans 8:28 and be pessimistic or downcast. Hope is full of optimism and joy. Remember, hope is a confident expectation of the goodness of God.

There are some wonderful verses in Scripture that reinforce this concept. One of them is found in Psalm 23:6. David says, "Surely goodness and mercy shall follow me all the days of my life, and I will dwell in the house of the Lord forever." I love that verse. Goodness and mercy are following my life. Goodness and mercy are following your life—not just when we get to heaven, but right now!

When I preach on this verse I like to say, "There are two angels that follow me everywhere I go. One is called Goodness, the other is called Mercy. Because I know they attend my footsteps, I dare to believe I can do what God has called me to do."

When I go into Baghdad, I believe that goodness and mercy are following me. They are protecting me. They are watching over me. I have a confident expectation of the goodness of God. You may protest and say, "Terry Law, are you saying that bad things do not happen to good people?"

No, I'm not saying that. I have seen bad things happen to very good people. I've experienced it in my own life. My wife, Jan, was killed in a car accident in Tulsa on September 28, 1982. I stood with my three children, watching her body being lowered into the ground. Yes, bad things happen to good people, but what brought me through the tragedy was strengthening my hope in God. I chose to believe that the bottom line in my life was God's goodness.

I still don't understand the reason for Jan's death. When I get to heaven, I'm going to talk to Jesus about it. But I still believe with all my heart that the bottom line of God in my life is goodness. I have a confident expectation of the goodness of God. And no matter what comes my way, He will work it for my good.

In Matthew 7:11 Jesus says, "If you then, being evil, know how to give good gifts to your children, how much more will your Father who is in heaven give good things to those who ask Him!" When you buy Christmas presents for your loved ones, particularly your children, do you go out of your way to find something bad, something they would not like? No, you carefully look around for things that you know they want. Then you wrap them and put them under a Christmas tree.

If we as carnal people know how to give good gifts to our children, Jesus reasons, how much more will He give good gifts—especially goodness and mercy—to us, His children? There's a powerful sermon in those three words, *how much more?* God is always the God of how much more. The thought is overwhelming. How much more will your Father who is in heaven give good things to those who ask Him? God wants to give you good things. Why? Because He is a good God. Remember, something *good* is going to happen to you.

James 1:17 says, "Every good gift and every perfect gift is from above, and comes down from the Father of lights, with whom there is no variation or shadow of turning." Every good gift comes from God. Goodness is His nature. Hope instills an expectation in us that goodness is coming our way.

Jeremiah 29:11 in the *King James Version* says, "For I know the thoughts that I think toward you, says the Lord, thoughts of peace [good] and not of evil, to give you a future and a hope." Those are the thoughts that God thinks toward you every day of your life. He is thinking thoughts of goodness, not of evil. He is planning to give you a future, a wonderful future.

Notice those final words, "and a hope." God has plans to give you hope (a confident expectation of His goodness toward you). You can't see these Scriptures in the Bible and not be filled with radiant hope in your heavenly Father.

In This Lifetime

In Psalm 103:1, David says, "Bless the Lord, O my soul; and all that is within me, bless His holy name!" Verses 4 and 5 say, "Who redeems your life from destruction, who crowns you with lovingkindness and tender mercies, who satisfies your mouth with good things so that your youth is renewed like the eagle's."

What a beautiful picture this is of God! I feel such anointing, even as I write these words. God crowns you with lovingkindness. Every day God extends His tender mercies toward you. He satisfies your mouth with good things. He's happy when you eat well.

I like this last phrase, "so that your youth is renewed like the eagle's." God is renewing my youth. I have a schedule that would keep a much younger man very busy. But I know in my heart of hearts that my youth is being renewed like the eagle's. I have strength because of my hope in God.

David says it well in Psalm 27:13: "I would have lost heart [despaired], unless I had believed that I would see the goodness of the Lord in the land of the living."

A lot of people say, "Oh, I'm going to see God's goodness when I get to heaven."

David said, "No, I'm going to see God's goodness in the land of the living." I agree with David and with God's Word. God's goodness is coming to me before I die. God's goodness is coming to me in this lifetime.

David said, "I would have lost hope." How do you lose hope? When you can't believe that God's goodness is coming to you. But praise God for the power of this verse. You and I will see the goodness of the Lord in the land of the living. Dare to declare this over your life!

Why is it important for us to review these verses? When we meditate on verses concerning the goodness of God, we are putting the helmet of hope on our heads. Remember, in 1 Thessalonians 5:8 Paul says, "But let us who are of the day be sober, putting on the breastplate of faith and love, and as a helmet the hope of salvation."

I refuse to despair because I am confident of God's goodness. I've had tragedies. I've seen bad things happen. But my hope is strong. In the midst of dark clouds, God is the shining light who is showing me the way, shaping me and molding me for my good. In the midst of trials, I can say that *something good is going to happen to me.*

Can I give you some personal advice? The first few moments when you awake in the morning are vital moments for the rest of the day. Nothing will better prepare you for a day than to put on your helmet of hope as soon as you wake up—when you dare to say with your mouth, "Surely goodness and mercy are going to follow me today. Something good is going to happen to me. God has plans for good and not for evil, to give me a future and a hope today." That's putting on the helmet of hope.

In 1 Peter 1:13 Peter says, "Therefore gird up the loins of your mind, be sober, and rest your hope fully upon the grace that is to be brought to you at the revelation of Jesus Christ." The *New American Standard Bible* says it this way: "Therefore, prepare your minds for action, keep sober in spirit, fix your hope completely on the grace to be brought to you at the revelation of Jesus Christ." Those are powerful words.

What grace will be brought to you at the revelation of Jesus Christ? Paul says you are to fix your hope completely on this event. I believe Paul is talking about the judgment seat of Christ, the time when Jesus will be fully revealed to all people. In 2 Corinthians 5:10, Paul says, "For we must all appear before the judgment seat of Christ." This event can give us hope because through the blood of Jesus we will be saved from God's wrath at the time of judgment. (See Rom. 5:9.) That is a great hope indeed!

God's Thank You

Most Christians are afraid of the subject of judgment in the Bible. They are afraid of that moment when their name is called and we stand before the *bema* seat,[1] or the judgment seat of Christ. We're afraid because we feel that God is going to rebuke us for all of our mistakes and all of our errors.

The enemy is constantly trying to make us feel guilty and condemned, dreading the moment when we stand before Jesus on the "day of judgment." He can get away with this if we don't understand that our sin has been blotted out by the blood of Jesus. God has no record of our sin. It has been remitted. God has applied His bulk eraser to all the sins of our lives. They do not exist anymore. And He has no knowledge of them.

The judgment seat of Christ is to reward us for our service. The judgment day is the day that God says, "Well done" to us and thanks us personally for what we have done in His kingdom. What will God reward us for? Many things.

He'll reward us for our hospitality. The Bible says that if we give a cup of cold water in the name of a disciple, we shall receive a reward. (See Matt. 10:42.) Even the little things, like taking kids to Sunday school, helping serve food at a church function, or going out of our way to serve our community by picking up trash on the road will be rewarded by God on that day.

What will God thank you for? For one thing, He'll say, "Thank you for giving to the poor." Angels take note when you do something special for them. James 1:27 says, "Pure and undefiled religion before God and the Father is this: to visit orphans and widows in their trouble."

When the angel came to Cornelius, he said, "Your prayers and your alms have come up as a memorial before God" (Acts 10:4). God made note that Cornelius gave to the poor. He's keeping a record, and there's coming a day when He's going to say, "Thanks." God will thank you for working faithfully in your job, using the talent that He's given you, and being a good steward of the time, the money, the energy, the intelligence, and the opportunities He gave you.

God will thank you for winning people to Christ: "Those who are wise shall shine like the brightness of the firmament [heavens], and those who turn many to righteousness like the stars forever and ever" (Dan. 12:3).

God will thank you for giving your hard-earned money to those who win the lost throughout the world, going to places you are not called to go. Just think of the people who will welcome you into heaven because of the investment you made in those who brought them the Good News. Every sacrificial gift that you plant in the kingdom will have its reward.

God will thank you for your prayers, for those uncounted moments when you knelt in the quietness of your bedroom or your study or over the kitchen sink, praying and talking to Him about your family, your church, or missionaries around the world.

God will thank you for standing strong in the midst of those things you never sought for or prayed for, but the enemy came in and attacked you with them, such as divorce and death. He will also thank you for being a doer of His Word in raising your children, fulfilling your call, and making innumerable sacrifices in life to see His kingdom advance in the earth.

God's greatest thank you will be to those who have been martyred for the sake of His kingdom. I have heard that one hundred and sixty-seven thousand believers across the globe gave their lives for the kingdom of God just in the year 2000.

Notice again in 1 Peter 1:13, Paul says, "Fix your hope completely on the grace that will be brought to you at the revelation of Jesus

Christ." God is waiting to say thank you to you! You are to fix your hope on the day. It's something to look forward to because through the blood of Jesus we have the solid hope that we will be rewarded.

In Titus 2:13 Paul writes, "Looking for the blessed hope, and glorious appearing of our great God and Savior Jesus Christ." What a powerful phrase, "the blessed hope." This hope releases you from the bondage of time. You are not a slave to the few years that you have to spend on the earth. You are looking forward to eternity with God. That is your ultimate hope!

Having this blessed hope has a tremendous effect on the way you live. The blessed hope liberates you from the fear of death, from the restrictions of time, and from the bondages that can come from the ever-changing circumstances of life. You are free to live the life God has called you to live to the fullest, giving your all to Him and His kingdom. It is not hard to understand, then, why the enemy has tried to keep believers from recognizing the importance and power of hope! It truly is our mind's strategic defense against his lies and deceptions.

CHAPTER 10

Hope: The Mind's Defense, Part 2

The helmet of salvation, your hope in God, is that powerful defense that covers your mind. Being saved means you live in the confident expectation of the goodness of God toward you. You know this because He tells you in His Word that He has a great future for you, that something good is going to happen to you today and every day, and that any bad things that happen will be worked to your good.

Not only do you have hope in this life, but also you have the blessed hope, the eternal hope of your salvation, which is spending eternity in heaven with Jesus. In 1 Corinthians 15:19 Paul says, "If in this life only we have hope in Christ, we are of all men the most pitiable."

Aren't you thankful for the fact that we have hope beyond the grave? Have you ever been to a funeral where people had no hope, where they grieved over a lost loved one and had no hope for their eternal welfare or confidence of seeing them again?

When I travel in Muslim nations, I am continually surprised to see the intensity of their grief at death. They will wail in high-pitched voices, sometimes trying to pull out their hair. Why? Because even though their religion teaches an afterlife, it is a false hope. It is not based on salvation through the blood of Jesus Christ. No matter how indoctrinated they are, in the end they face death with no helmet of salvation. They instinctively know there is no hope for them or their loved ones in death.

Thank God, we have the real hope of eternal life. In 1 Thessalonians 4:13, Paul says, "But I do not want you to be ignorant, brethren, concerning those who have fallen asleep, lest you sorrow as others who have no hope." Those who have no hope sorrow, and there's no answer for the sorrow. Hopelessness is the saddest human condition possible.

Paul talks about this condition in Ephesians 2:12: "At that time you were without Christ, being aliens from the commonwealth of Israel and strangers from the covenants of promise, having no hope and without God in the world." Notice the words "having no hope and without God in the world."

One thing I've learned about hope through the years is that hope grows strong through testing. Romans 5:2 says, "Through whom also we have access by faith into this grace in which we stand, and rejoice in hope of the glory of God." That word *rejoice* means to exult; it indicates a confident boasting.[1] We can boast confidently in our hope of the glory of God.

Paul boasted about the glory of God that was awaiting him. In verses 3-5 he says, "And not only that, but we also glory in tribulations, knowing that tribulation produces perseverance, and perseverance character, and character hope. Now hope does not disappoint."

In verse 3 Paul says, "We also glory in tribulations." "Glory" is translated from the same Greek word used for *rejoice;* it means we exult—we confidently boast in tribulation. How do you react to tribulation and trials in your life?

I remember when I traveled with Oral Roberts in the last days of his crusades. His crusade director was Bob DeWeese. One day in a crusade a lady came forward and asked Mr. DeWeese to pray for her. He said, "What do you want?"

She said, "I want you to pray that God will give me patience."

Bob placed his hand on her head and said, "O Lord, I pray that You'll give her tribulation."

She grabbed his hand and took it off her head, saying, "No, don't pray that. I asked you to pray for patience."

So Bob placed his hand on her head one more time and said, "O Lord, give her tribulation."

By this time she was quite irate. Again she pulled his hand off her head and said, "Why are you praying that?"

He pointed out to her that in Scripture the Bible says, "Tribulation worketh patience," or perseverance.

There's something about going through the trials of life that does something to your hope. When you've seen God come through in the hard times, when you've looked death or difficulty squarely in the face and come through, having your hope in the goodness of God, it produces patience and perseverance, and out of that perseverance comes proven character.

Always remember: Hope has to be tested by tribulation in order to be proved genuine and strong. When you get that kind of hope, you won't be disappointed.

Rejoice in your trials. Why? Your hope is getting stronger. What is your hope? It's a confident expectation of the goodness of God. It's believing that something good is going to happen to you. If you stay with it and keep putting on the helmet of salvation, you'll have a strong, confident, radiant, and unshakable hope in God.

An Anchor of the Soul

There is another powerful picture of hope in Hebrews 6:18-20: "That by two immutable things in which it is impossible for God to lie, we might have a strong consolation, who have fled for refuge to lay hold upon the hope set before us. This hope we have as an anchor of the soul, both sure and steadfast, and which enters the Presence behind the veil. Where the forerunner has entered for us, even Jesus, having become High Priest forever according to the order of Melchizedek."

The writer of Hebrews tells us that when we flee for refuge, we are to lay hold of the hope set before us. He says that this hope is an anchor of our souls. In one short sentence, he gives us a powerful picture of hope. Hope is an anchor.

What needs an anchor? There's only one thing that I know of that needs an anchor, and that's a boat or a ship. Why does a boat need an anchor? Because it is floating on water. Water is a totally unstable element. Water is moving all the time. If you were to stick your hand into water and try to grab a handful, when you came up there'd be no water in your hand. There's nothing in water that you can fasten onto; it is totally unstable.

This is a powerful picture of life itself. Our life is like water. Life is impermanent. It is unstable. It is always moving and changing. Our financial affairs are always changing. There are constant physical changes going on in our bodies. Our relationships are continuously growing stronger or weaker. So it is with water. Water is moving, it's unstable, you can't depend on it. It's here, and it's there, and then it passes away.

There are times in life when the water is whipped into a storm. It's amazing what wind can do to water. In 1965 I traveled overseas in a ship from Montreal, Canada, to Cape Town, South Africa— twenty-eight days across the open Atlantic. I will never forget the power of the wind on the water. There were times that the waves rose so high, I did not know how we were going to escape alive.

Life is like that. The storms come. It looks like your ship is going to the bottom. There's only one thing that will give you safety and security, and that is an anchor. Like every boat, you have got to have an anchor. The anchor passes through the unstable water, through that element that is always moving and changing, and fastens onto a rock or the earth. It is only with an anchor that a boat is secure and stable.

In the storms of life, we've got to have an anchor, something that grabs on and holds firm. When it looks like the storm is going to overwhelm us, Hebrews 6:19 says that we have an anchor. What is our anchor? "This hope we have as an anchor of the soul, both sure and steadfast."

Your hope in God is your anchor in life. Your hope is the assurance that you're going to get through the storm. Your hope is the assurance that something good is going to happen to you. Your hope is the confident expectation that all things are working together for good.

Notice now, in this picture of hope, that it says that our hope is like an anchor that enters the presence of God behind the veil in heaven. Verse 20 says, "Where the forerunner has entered for us, even Jesus, having become a High Priest."

Hundreds of years ago the captain of every ship knew the dangers of the sea. The greatest danger was coming into a port or a harbor that he did not know. If he came into a harbor in a storm, in a fog, or with the wind blowing strongly, he needed to know where the rocks were, where the shoals and the reefs were hidden. And so the captain of the ship would summon the forerunner.

Every ship had a forerunner. A forerunner was a man who was an expert swimmer. He would tie a very light rope around his waist. They knew the harbor was up ahead, but they didn't know where to anchor the boat. So the forerunner would dive off the boat into the water, swim through the water, and find out where the reefs and the rocks and the dangerous spots were. When he found the right spot to anchor the boat, he would tug on the line.

Then, with all of his strength, he would pull the anchor over to the spot and fasten it. The captain was sure that the boat would never be smashed on the rocks because the anchor that held the boat was secure.

What a powerful picture we have here of Jesus Christ! The Bible says that He is our Forerunner. He has gone into the presence of God and fastened our anchor to the Rock. He is our High Priest. When He died on the cross and rose from the dead, He dove into the waters of life.

When He ascended to the right hand of the Father, He took the anchor of hope with Him. He is now seated at the right hand of the Father. He is always interceding on our behalf. He never sleeps. He's never going to die. He's living forever.

He's my personal Representative, offering my prayers to the Father. And my anchor, my hope, is fastened to the Rock. He is the Rock. His Word is my Rock. My eternity is secure because my hope is anchored to the Rock.

Dare to believe it today, in the storms of your life: your hope is your anchor; something good is going to happen to you. Dare to have a confident expectation in the goodness of God. You're going to make it. You're not going under; you're going over.

We have an anchor that keeps the soul, steadfast and sure while the billows roll. Anchored to the rock that cannot move. Anchored firm and deep in the Savior's love.

This old hymn of the church tells the story of our hope. Will your anchor hold in the storms of life? That's a good question. I know mine will. Why? Because my anchor is hope in God, and He tells me that something good is going to happen to me.

Abound in Hope

First Corinthians 13:13 gives us the powerful threefold chord of our walk with God: faith, hope, and love. Let me ask you a question. Is God a God of faith? Yes, Hebrews 11:3 says that by faith God formed the worlds. Is God a God of love? Yes, 1 John 4:8 tells us that God is love. The question now comes: Is God also a God of hope? Romans 15:13 tells us the truth: "Now may the God of hope fill you with all joy and peace in believing, that you may abound in hope by the power of the Holy Spirit."

What a powerful declaration this verse makes! Your God is a God of hope. Think of it. God has a plan for you. He wants you to abound in hope.

Some people have never dared to believe this about God. They've always thought God was full of judgment, that He wanted to get even with them, that He was waiting for them to trip up so that He could pounce on them. That is not the picture of God that we see in the Bible. He is the God of hope; He is the God of something good is going to happen to you.

Paul says, "May the God of hope fill you with all joy and peace in believing." Would you like to have joy and peace? Did you know God wants to fill you with joy and peace? How does God do that? The answer is found in this verse, but before I share it with you, I want to show you something and make a suggestion.

The words in Scripture are inspired by the Holy Spirit; however, in Old Testament Hebrew and New Testament Greek, there was no punctuation in the original manuscripts. Therefore, in your Bible the periods and the commas are not inspired. They were not there in the original version. The periods and commas in your Bible were put there by the translators.

In Romans 15:13 I believe they put the comma in the wrong place. The comma is after the word *believing*. When you read the verse, it says, "Now may the God of hope fill you with all joy and peace in believing, [comma] that you may abound in hope by the power of the Holy Spirit." So I suggest that you move the comma from after the word *believing* and put it after the word *peace*. Now the verse reads, "Now may the God of hope fill you with all joy and peace, in believing that you may abound in hope by the power of the Holy Spirit."

How does God fill you with all joy and peace? God fills you with joy and peace when you dare to believe that you may abound in hope by the power of the Holy Spirit!

Do you see what I'm saying here? As you read this book, as you meditate on these words right now, dare to believe that when you put this book down you may abound in hope by the power of the Holy Spirit. That is one of the most liberating, empowering phrases in the entire Bible.

Will you dare to believe that you will abound in hope? What does "abound" mean? Abound means to overflow, to have more than enough, bubbling up and over. In other words, you have so much hope that you don't know what to do with it all.

What do people think about you when they talk to you? Do people like to be around you? Do people enjoy your personality? What do you say to people when they ask, "How are you doing?" Do you give them an organ recital, telling them what's wrong with your heart, your liver, and the other organs of the body? Or do you recite the great works of God in your life and tell of His love and goodness toward you?

Hope is one of the most infectious qualities you possess in Christ. Paul says, "May the God of hope fill you with abounding hope," which is so much hope you don't know what to do with it; so much hope that when people who are despairing see you, your hope rubs off on them. Your hope bubbles up, inspires them, and makes them feel better about their lives.

God wants us to have more hope than we know what to do with, more hope than we need to meet our own needs, for a reason. We have abundant hope to minister to others. In a hopeless world, in a world where so many people have no hope in God, we are the answer. Our overflow of hope brings hope to others.

You can abound in hope. Paul is saying, "If you dare to believe that you can abound in hope by the power of the Holy Spirit, then your life is going to be different. When others around you are discouraged, downcast, and beaten up; when they come to you in desperation, you will have a word of hope for them."

When they say, "How are you doing?" you say, "Surely goodness and mercy are following me all the days of my life. Something good is happening to me. God has a plan for me, a plan for good and not for evil, to give me a future and a hope—and He will do the same for you if you just trust Him."

Put On God's Helmet

Satan fires his thoughts at us like fiery darts. We are subject to random thoughts coming from nowhere. But God has given us heavenly protection. There is defensive armor that will help you weather the storms of life. And the one piece of defensive armor that protects your mind and your thoughts is the helmet of hope. Let me say it again: Just because you're born again doesn't mean that you have put on the helmet.

Why is there so much depression, worry, fear, and pessimism in the church today? It's because we've forgotten this message. This is the forgotten message of God to the church today: Put on the helmet of the hope of salvation!

There are Scriptures on hope in the Bible that you need to get hold of. I've listed some of them for you in the next section, in addition to some on God's goodness and His blessings. Read them. Memorize them. Meditate on them. Speak them whenever you have the opportunity. This is how you will retrain your mind to be anchored in the hope of your salvation; that God has something good for you today, tomorrow, and for eternity.

It may take you a while, but I promise you that if you put on your helmet of salvation, if you meditate on these Scriptures, you will become a Bible-believing optimist and conquer every thought attack Satan wields against your mind and heart.

This is my benediction to you: *Now may the God of hope fill you with all joy and peace, in believing that you may abound in hope by the power of the Holy Spirit.*

Conclusion

This book was birthed out of a desire to see believers maintain victory in their walk with God. Every day the enemy assails us with thought attacks that seek to erect strongholds of defeat in our minds. But God has not left us helpless! In 2 Corinthians 10:4 KJV, Paul declares, "The weapons of our warfare are not carnal but [they are] mighty through God to the pulling down of strong holds." God has given us mighty weapons by which we can overcome.

In this book you have seen the mind games that Satan plays in your life. His *modus operandi* hasn't changed since the original temptation of Adam and Eve in the Garden. And even though you are a child of God, you are still subject to the suggestions of the evil one. You hear him when he tells you that you will never be good enough; that you're so weak; that you're always making mistakes; that if you think about a sin, it's just as bad as doing it, so you might as well go ahead and sin. He tells you that you will never pay your bills on time, that your children will backslide and fall away from God, and he throws mental roadblocks into the path of your having a good marriage. In general, he assaults your mind in order to kill, steal, and destroy.

You have also studied your weapons and learned how to use them. There will be parts of this book that will speak to your specific situation. I counsel you to go back and study the book again and again until you are operating in faith in the particular area where you need it. If God is convicting you of something in your life, then repent; change your way of thinking; go in a new direction.

This is key: Use the power of the Word against temptation. Use the power of the Name against deception. Use the power of the Blood against accusation.

Remember that you have been made the righteousness of God in Christ. God has made you one with Himself through the blood of Jesus. You are a child of God, an heir of all His blessings. It's one thing to mentally comprehend the doctrine of righteousness; it's another thing entirely to get the revelation of it in your heart.

Go back and meditate on your righteousness in Christ until the reality of it explodes inside your spirit. The one way to be sure that this happens is to use your mouth as the launching pad that God meant it to be. Dare to say with your mouth everything that the Word says about you. Remember, "With the mouth confession is made unto all the blessings of salvation."

Finally, every morning when you get out of bed, put on your helmet of salvation, the anchor of hope. In those first few moments as you awake, get into the habit of thinking God's thoughts. Say with your mouth: "Surely goodness and mercy will follow me through this entire day." "God has a plan for me today, a plan for good and not for evil, to give me a future and a hope." "Something good is going to happen to me today."

Let me close with these final words. The truths in this book are eternal. They are the answer you need to overcome in your walk with God. Meditate on these truths; let the Holy Spirit reveal them to your spirit. My prayer for you is the prayer that Paul prayed for the church in Ephesus: "that the God of our Lord Jesus Christ, the Father of glory, may give to you the spirit of wisdom and revelation in the knowledge of Him, the eyes of your understanding being enlightened; that you may know what is the hope of His calling, what are the riches of the glory of His inheritance in the saints" (Eph. 1:17,18). May the Holy Spirit open your inner eyes to the power of this revelation. Amen.

Scriptures

New Testament Hope—The Confident Expectation of God's Goodness

1 Corinthians 13:13: And now abide faith, *hope,* love, these three; but the greatest of these is love.

Romans 8:28: And we know that all things work together for good to those who love God, to those who are the called according to His purpose.

1 Thessalonians 5:8: But let us who are of the day be sober, putting on the breastplate of faith and love, and as a helmet the *hope* of salvation.

Psalm 23:6: Surely goodness and mercy shall follow me all the days of my life; And I will dwell in the house of the Lord forever.

Psalm 27:13: I would have lost heart, unless I had believed that I would see the goodness of the Lord in the land of the living.

Psalm 107:8-9 (AMP): Oh, that men would praise [and confess to] the Lord for His goodness and loving-kindness and His wonderful works to the children of men! For He satisfies the longing soul and fills the hungry soul with good.

Psalm 103:1-5: Bless the Lord, O my soul; And all that is within me, bless His holy name! Bless the Lord, O my soul, And forget not all His benefits: Who forgives all your iniquities, Who heals all your diseases, Who redeems your life from destruction, Who crowns you with lovingkindness and tender mercies, Who satisfies your mouth with good things, So that your youth is renewed like the eagle's.

Jeremiah 29:11 (NIV): "For I know the plans I have for you," declares the Lord, "plans to prosper you and not to harm you, plans to give you *hope* and a future."

Romans 15:13: Now may the God of *hope* fill you with all joy and peace in believing, that you may abound in *hope* by the power of the Holy Spirit.

Romans 15:4: For whatever things were written before were written for our learning, that we through the patience and comfort of the Scriptures might have *hope*.

Hebrews 10:23: Let us hold fast the confession of our *hope* without wavering, for He who promised is faithful.

Acts 26:6-7: And now I stand and am judged for the *hope* of the promise made by God to our fathers. To this promise our twelve tribes, earnestly serving God night and day, *hope* to attain. For this *hope's* sake, King Agrippa, I am accused by the Jews.

Romans 4:17-18: (as it is written, "I have made you a father of many nations") in the presence of Him whom he believed—God, who gives life to the dead and calls those things which do not exist as though they did; who, contrary to *hope*, in *hope* believed, so that he became the father of many nations, according to what was spoken, "So shall your descendants be."

Romans 5:3-5: And not only that, but we also glory in tribulations, knowing that tribulation produces perseverance; and perseverance, character; and character, *hope*. Now *hope* does not disappoint, because the love of God has been poured out in our hearts by the Holy Spirit who was given to us.

Romans 8:24-25: For we were saved in this *hope*, but *hope* that is seen is not *hope*; for why does one still *hope* for what he sees? But if we *hope* for what we do not see, we eagerly wait for it with perseverance.

2 Corinthians 10:15 (AMP): We do not boast therefore, beyond our proper limit, over other men's labors, but we have the *hope* and confident expectation that as your faith continues to grow, our field among you may be greatly enlarged, still within the limits of our commission.

Galatians 5:5 (AMP): For we, [not relying on the Law but] through the [Holy] Spirit's [help], by faith anticipate and wait for the blessing and good for which our righteousness and right standing with God [our conformity to His will in purpose, thought, and action, causes us] to *hope*.

Ephesians 1:18: the eyes of your understanding being enlightened; that you may know what is the *hope* of His calling, what are the riches of the glory of His inheritance in the saints.

Ephesians 2:12: that at that time you were without Christ, being aliens from the commonwealth of Israel and strangers from the covenants of promise, having no *hope* and without God in the world.

Ephesians 4:4 (AMP): [There is] one body and one Spirit—just as there is also one *hope* [that belongs] to the calling you received.

Colossians 1:3-5 (AMP): We continually give thanks to God the Father of our Lord Jesus Christ (the Messiah), as we are praying for you, For we have heard of your faith in Christ Jesus [the leaning of your entire human personality on Him in absolute trust and confidence in His power, wisdom, and goodness] and of the love which you [have and show] for all the saints (God's consecrated ones), Because of the *hope* [of experiencing what is] laid up (reserved and waiting) for you in heaven. Of this [*hope*] you heard in the past in the message of the truth of the Gospel.

Colossians 1:26-27: the mystery which has been hidden from ages and from generations, but now has been revealed to His saints. To them God willed to make known what are the riches of the glory of this mystery among the Gentiles: which is Christ in you, the *hope* of glory.

Colossians 1:23: if indeed you continue in the faith, grounded and steadfast, and are not moved away from the *hope* of the gospel which you heard, which was preached to every creature under heaven, of which I, Paul, became a minister.

1 Thessalonians 1:3: remembering without ceasing your work of faith, labor of love, and patience of *hope* in our Lord Jesus Christ in the sight of our God and Father.

1 Thessalonians 2:19: For what is our *hope*, or joy, or crown of rejoicing? Is it not even you in the presence of our Lord Jesus Christ at His coming?

1 Thessalonians 4:13: But I do not want you to be ignorant, brethren, concerning those who have fallen asleep, lest you sorrow as others who have no *hope*.

1 Timothy 1:1: Paul, an apostle of Jesus Christ, by the commandment of God our Savior and the Lord Jesus Christ, our *hope*.

1 Timothy 4:9-10 (NIV): This is a trustworthy saying that deserves full acceptance (and for this we labor and strive), that we have put our *hope* in the living God, who is the Savior of all men, and especially of those who believe.

1 Timothy 5:5 (NIV): The widow who is really in need and left all alone puts her *hope* in God and continues night and day to pray and to ask God for help.

1 Timothy 6:17 (NIV): Command those who are rich in this present world not to be arrogant nor to put their *hope* in wealth, which is so uncertain, but to put their *hope* in God, who richly provides us with everything for our enjoyment.

Titus 1:2: in *hope* of eternal life which God, who cannot lie, promised before time began.

Titus 2:13: looking for the blessed *hope* and glorious appearing of our great God and Savior Jesus Christ.

Hebrews 3:6: but Christ as a Son over His own house, whose house we are if we hold fast the confidence and the rejoicing of the *hope* firm to the end.

Hebrews 6:18-20: that by two immutable things, in which it is impossible for God to lie, we might have strong consolation, who have fled for refuge to lay hold of the *hope* set before us. This *hope* we have as an anchor of the soul, both sure and steadfast, and which enters the Presence behind the veil, where the forerunner has entered for us, even Jesus, having become High Priest forever according to the order of Melchizedek.

1 Peter 1:3: Blessed be the God and Father of our Lord Jesus Christ, who according to His abundant mercy has begotten us again to a living *hope* through the resurrection of Jesus Christ from the dead.

1 Peter 1:13 (AMP): So brace up your minds; be sober (circumspect, morally alert); set your *hope* wholly and unchangeably on the grace (divine favor) that is coming to you when Jesus Christ (the Messiah) is revealed.

1 Peter 3:15: But sanctify the Lord God in your hearts, and always be ready to give a defense to everyone who asks you a reason for the *hope* that is in you, with meekness and fear.

1 John 3:2-3: Beloved, now we are children of God; and it has not yet been revealed what we shall be, but we know that when He is revealed, we shall be like Him, for we shall see Him as He is. And everyone who has this *hope* in Him purifies himself, just as He is pure.

1 Corinthians 15:19: If in this life only we have *hope* in Christ, we are of all men the most pitiable.

Hebrews 11:1: Now faith is the substance of things *hoped* for, the evidence of things not seen.

2 Corinthians 1:10 (NIV): He has delivered us from such a deadly peril, and he will deliver us. On him we have set our *hope* that he will continue to deliver us.

Two Adjectives That Describe Hope— Good and Blessed

More Verses on Hope

Hope (Greek: *elpis*[1]) — To anticipate with pleasure.[2]

Psalm 16:9: Therefore my heart is glad, and my glory rejoices; My flesh also will rest in *hope*.

Jeremiah 17:13: O Lord, the *hope* of Israel, All who forsake You shall be ashamed. "Those who depart from Me Shall be written in the earth, Because they have forsaken the Lord, The fountain of living waters."

Psalm 119:116: Uphold me according to Your word, that I may live; And do not let me be ashamed of my *hope*.

2 Corinthians 3:12: Therefore, since we have such *hope*, we use great boldness of speech.

Psalm 42:11: Why are you cast down, O my soul? And why are you disquieted within me? *Hope* in God; For I shall yet praise Him, The help of my countenance and my God.

Proverbs 13:12: *Hope* deferred makes the heart sick, But when the desire comes, it is a tree of life.

Psalm 146:5: Happy is he who has the God of Jacob for his help, Whose *hope* is in the Lord his God.

Jeremiah 14:8: O the *Hope* of Israel, his Savior in time of trouble, Why should You be like a stranger in the land, And like a traveler who turns aside to tarry for a night?

Jeremiah 17:7: "Blessed is the man who trusts in the Lord And whose *hope* is the Lord."

Jeremiah 31:17: There is *hope* in your future, says the Lord, That your children shall come back to their own border.

Lamentations 3:21-26: This I recall to my mind, Therefore I have *hope*. Through the Lord's mercies we are not consumed, Because His compassions fail not. They are new every morning; Great is Your faithfulness. "The Lord is my portion," says my soul, "Therefore I *hope* in Him!" The Lord is good to those who wait for Him, To the soul who seeks Him. It is good that one should *hope* and wait quietly For the salvation of the Lord.

Psalm 31:24: Be of good courage, And He shall strengthen your heart, All you who *hope* in the Lord.

Psalm 33:18: Behold, the eye of the Lord is on those who fear Him, On those who *hope* in His mercy.

Psalm 42:5: Why are you cast down, O my soul? And why are you disquieted within me? *Hope* in God, for I shall yet praise Him for the help of His countenance.

Psalm 71:14: But I will *hope* continually, And will praise You yet more and more.

Psalm 119:81: My soul faints for Your salvation, But I *hope* in Your word.

Hope is a confident expectation of the *Goodness* of God

God's Goodness

Genesis 50:20 (AMP): As for you, you thought evil against me, but God meant it for *good*, to bring about that many people should be kept alive, as they are this day.

Numbers 10:29: Now Moses said to Hobab son of Reuel the Midianite, Moses' father-in-law, "We are setting out for the place about which the Lord said, 'I will give it to you.' Come with us and we will treat you well, for the Lord has promised *good* things to Israel."

Psalm 34:8: Oh, taste and see that the Lord is *good*; Blessed is the man who trusts in Him!

Isaiah 1:19: If you are willing and obedient, You shall eat the *good* of the land.

Acts 10:38: how God anointed Jesus of Nazareth with the Holy Spirit and with power, who went about doing *good* and healing all who were oppressed by the devil, for God was with Him.

1 Kings 8:56: "Blessed be the Lord, who has given rest to His people Israel, according to all that He promised. There has not failed one word of all His *good* promise, which He promised through His servant Moses."

John 10:11: "I am the *good* shepherd. The *good* shepherd gives His life for the sheep."

Psalm 85:12: Yes, the Lord will give what is *good*; And our land will yield its increase.

Psalm 84:11: For the Lord God is a sun and shield; The Lord will give grace and glory; No *good* thing will He withhold from those who walk uprightly.

Joshua 23:14: "Behold, this day I am going the way of all the earth. And you know in all your hearts and in all your souls that not one thing has failed of all the *good* things which the Lord your God spoke concerning you. All have come to pass for you; not one word of them has failed."

Isaiah 61:1: The Spirit of the Lord God is upon Me, Because the Lord has anointed Me to preach *good* tidings to the poor; He has sent Me to heal the brokenhearted, To proclaim liberty to the captives, And the opening of the prison to those who are bound.

Philippians 1:6: being confident of this very thing, that He who has begun a *good* work in you will complete it until the day of Jesus Christ.

Exodus 33:18-19: And he said, "Please, show me Your glory." Then He said, "I will make all My *goodness* pass before you, and I will proclaim the name of the Lord before you. I will be gracious to whom I will be gracious, and I will have compassion on whom I will have compassion."

Psalm 65:11 (AMP): You crown the year with Your bounty and *good -ness,* and the tracks of Your [chariot wheels] drip with fatness.

Psalm 107:20: He sent His word and healed them, And delivered them from their destructions.

Jeremiah 31:14: "and My people shall be satisfied with My *good - ness,* says the Lord."

Zechariah 9:17: For how great is its *goodness* And how great its beauty! Grain shall make the young men thrive, And new wine the young women.

Romans 2:4: Or do you despise the riches of His *goodness,* forbearance, and longsuffering, not knowing that the *goodness* of God leads you to repentance?

Mark 10:18: So Jesus said to him, "Why do you call Me *good?* No one is *good* but One, that is, God."

God's Blessings

Exaltation, Health, Reproductiveness, Prosperity, Victory, God's Favor

Deuteronomy 28:1-2: "Now it shall come to pass, if you diligently obey the voice of the Lord your God, to observe carefully all His commandments which I command you today, that the Lord your God will set you high above all nations of the earth. And all these *bless - ings* shall come upon you and overtake you, because you obey the voice of the Lord your God."

Galatians 3:13-14: Christ has redeemed us from the curse of the law, having become a curse for us (for it is written, "Cursed is everyone who hangs on a tree"), that the *blessing* of Abraham might come upon the Gentiles in Christ Jesus, that we might receive the promise of the Spirit through faith.

Isaiah 54:17: No weapon formed against you shall prosper, And every tongue which rises against you in judgment You shall condemn. This is the heritage of the servants of the Lord, And their righteousness is from Me," Says the Lord.

Psalm 118:17: I shall not die, but live, And declare the works of the Lord.

1 Peter 2:24: who Himself bore our sins in His own body on the tree, that we, having died to sins, might live for righteousness—by whose stripes you were healed.

Deuteronomy 29:29: "The secret things belong to the Lord our God, but those things which are revealed belong to us and to our children forever, that we may do all the words of this law."

Deuteronomy 33:25-27: Your sandals shall be iron and bronze; As your days, so shall your strength be. "There is no one like the God of Jeshurun, Who rides the heavens to help you, And in His excellency on the clouds. The eternal God is your refuge, And underneath are the everlasting arms; He will thrust out the enemy from before you, And will say, 'Destroy!'"

2 Corinthians 9:8: And God is able to make all grace abound toward you, that you, always having all sufficiency in all things, may have an abundance for every good work.

2 Timothy 1:7: For God has not given us a spirit of fear, but of power and of love and of a sound mind.

Genesis 1:22: And God *blessed* them, saying, "Be fruitful and multiply, and fill the waters in the seas, and let birds multiply on the earth."

Genesis 5:2: He created them male and female, and *blessed* them and called them Mankind in the day they were created.

Genesis 9:1: So God *blessed* Noah and his sons, and said to them: "Be fruitful and multiply, and fill the earth."

Genesis 12:2-3: "I will make you a great nation; I will *bless* you And make your name great; And you shall be a *blessing*. I will *bless* those who *bless* you, And I will curse him who curses you; And in you all the families of the earth shall be *blessed*."

Genesis 17:16: "And I will *bless* her and also give you a son by her; then I will *bless* her, and she shall be a mother of nations; kings of peoples shall be from her."

Numbers 6:24-26: "'The Lord *bless* you and keep you; The Lord make His face shine upon you, And be gracious to you; The Lord lift up His countenance upon you, And give you peace.'"

Galatians 3:29: And if you are Christ's, then you are Abraham's seed, and heirs according to the promise.

1 Chronicles 29:11-12: Yours, O Lord, is the greatness, The power and the glory, The victory and the majesty; For all that is in heaven and in earth is Yours; Yours is the kingdom, O Lord, And You are exalted as head over all. Both riches and honor come from You, And You reign over all. In Your hand is power and might; In Your hand it is to make great And to give strength to all.

Job 5:10-11: He gives rain on the earth, And sends waters on the fields. He sets on high those who are lowly, And those who mourn are lifted to safety.

Psalm 65:9-11: You visit the earth and water it, You greatly enrich it; The river of God is full of water; You provide their grain, For so You have prepared it. You water its ridges abundantly, You settle its furrows; You make it soft with showers, You *bless* its growth. You crown the year with Your goodness, And Your paths drip with abundance.

Deuteronomy 7:13-14: And He will love you and *bless* you and multiply you; He will also *bless* the fruit of your womb and the fruit of your land, your grain and your new wine and your oil, the increase of your cattle and the offspring of your flock, in the land of which He swore to your fathers to give you. You shall be *blessed* above all peoples; there shall not be a male or female barren among you or among your livestock.

Exodus 23:25-26: "So you shall serve the Lord your God, and He will *bless* your bread and your water. And I will take sickness away from the midst of you. No one shall suffer miscarriage or be barren in your land; I will fulfill the number of your days."

Exodus 15:26: "If you diligently heed the voice of the Lord your God and do what is right in His sight, give ear to His commandments and keep all His statutes, I will put none of the diseases on you which I have brought on the Egyptians. For I am the Lord who heals you."

Deuteronomy 28:1: "Now it shall come to pass, if you diligently obey the voice of the Lord your God, to observe carefully all His commandments which I command you today, that the Lord your God will set you high above all nations of the earth."

Isaiah 61:7: Instead of your shame you shall have double honor, And instead of confusion they shall rejoice in their portion. Therefore in their land they shall possess double; Everlasting joy shall be theirs.

Jeremiah 32:40-41 (NIV): I will make an everlasting covenant with them: I will never stop doing good to them, and I will inspire them to fear me, so that they will never turn away from me. I will rejoice in doing them good and will assuredly plant them in this land with all my heart and soul.

Deuteronomy 30:19: I call heaven and earth as witnesses today against you, that I have set before you life and death, *blessing* and cursing; therefore choose life, that both you and your descendants may live.

2 Samuel 7:29: "Now therefore, let it please You to *bless* the house of Your servant, that it may continue before You forever; for You, O Lord God, have spoken it, and with Your *blessing* let the house of Your servant be *blessed* forever."

Ezekiel 34:26: I will make them and the places all around My hill a *blessing;* and I will cause showers to come down in their season; there shall be showers of *blessing.*

Endnotes

Introduction

[1] Spiritual strongholds are spirit beings who make it their business to try to invade and wreck your life the moment you decide to serve God.

Chapter 1

[1] *Jamieson, Fausset, and Brown Commentary* electronic database (copyright © 1997 by Biblesoft), "Daniel 10:20." All rights reserved.

[2] Thayer and Smith, *The KJV New Testament Greek Lexicon*, "Greek Lexicon entry for noema," s.v. "thought," 2 Corinthians 10:5. Available from <http://www.biblestudytools.net/Lexicons/Greek/grk.cgi?number=3540&version=kjv>.

[3] Ibid., s.v. "device," 2 Corinthians 2:11.

[4] Ibid., s.v. "minds," 2 Corinthians 11:3.

[5] Michael Crichton, *Newsweek* magazine, "Greater Expectations," September 24, 1990, p. 58, Vol. 116, Issue 13.

Chapter 2

[1] James E. Strong, "Hebrew Chaldee Dictionary" in *Strong's Exhaustive Concordance of the Bible* (Nashville: Abingdon, 1890), p. 113, entry #7725, s.v. "repent," 1 Kings 8:47.

[2] Brown, Driver, Briggs and Gesenius, *The KJV Old Testament Hebrew Lexicon*, "Hebrew Lexicon entry for Ya`aqob," s.v. "Jacob," Genesis 25:26. Available from <http://www.biblestudytools.net/Lexicons/Hebrew/heb.cgi?number=3290&version=kjv>.

[3] Ibid., "Greek Dictionary of the New Testament," p. 47, entry #3338, s.v. "remorse," Mathew 27:3.

[4] Phillip Yancey, *What's So Amazing About Grace* (Grand Rapids, Michigan: Zondervan, 1997), p. 177.

[5] Ibid., pp. 179-180.

Chapter 3

[1] James E. Strong, "Greek Dictionary of the New Testament," p. 45, entry #3056, s.v. "word," John 1:1.

[2] Ibid., p. 45, entry #3056, s.v. "word," Hebrews 4:12.

[3] Ibid., p. 35, entry #2222, s.v. "life," John 1:4.

[4] Thayer and Smith, *The KJV New Testament Greek Lexicon*, "Greek Lexicon entry for *Zoe*," available from <http://www.biblestudytools.net/Lexicons/Greek/grk.cgi?number=2222&version=kjv>.

[5] Strong's, "Greek Dictionary of the New Testament," p. 35, entry #2222, s.v. "life," John 6:63.

[6] Ibid., p. 59, entry #4151, s.v. "spirit," John 6:63.

[7] Ibid., p. 59, entry #4151, s.v. "spirit," John 4:24.

[8] Ibid., p. 35, entry #2222, s.v. "life," 1 Peter 2:3.

[9] Ibid., p. 63, entry #4487, s.v. "nothing," Luke 1:37.

[10] Ibid., p. 63, entry #4487, s.v. "word," Romans 10:17.

[11] Ibid., p. 63, entry #4487, s.v. "word," Matthew 4:4.

[12] Ibid., p. 75, entry #5349, s.v. "corruptible," 1 Peter 1:23.

[13] Ibid., p. 17, entry #862, s.v. "incorruptible," 1 Peter 1:23.

[14] Brown, Driver, Briggs and Gesenius, "Hebrew Lexicon entry for Ruwach," s.v. "spirit," Psalm 33:6. Available from <http://www.biblestudytools.net/Lexicons/Hebrew/heb.cgi?number=7307&version=kjv>.

[15] Thayer and Smith, "Greek Lexicon entry for Energes, s.v. "powerful," Hebrews 4:12. Available from <http://www.biblestudytools.net/Lexicons/Greek/grk.cgi?number=1756&version=kjv>.

Chapter 5

[1] James E. Strong, "The New Strong's Complete Dictionary of Bible Words," p. 675, entry #3875, s.v. "parakletos."

Chapter 6

[1] *There Is Power in the Blood,* words and music by Lewis E. Jones, 1899. Available from <http://www.cyberhymnal.org>.

[2] Based on information from Thayer and Smith, "Greek Lexicon entries for Psuche, *Zoe*, Bios," s.v. "life." Available from <http://bible.crosswalk.com/Lexicons/NewTestamentGreek/grk.cgi?sarch=life&version=kjv&type=eng&submit=Find>.

[3] Brown, Driver, Briggs and Gesenius, "Hebrew Lexicon entry for Nephesh, s.v. "soul," Genesis 2:7. Available from <http://www.biblestudytools.net/ L e x i c o n s/Hebrew/heb.cgi?number=5315&version=kjv>.

[4] Ibid., Isaiah 53:12.

Chapter 8

[1] Brown, Driver, Briggs and Gesenius, "Hebrew Lexicon entry for Tselem, s.v. "image," Genesis 1:26. Available from <http://www.biblestudytools.net/Lexicons/Hebrew/heb.cgi?number=6754&version=kjv>.

[2] Based on information from Brown, Driver, Briggs and Gesenius, "Hebrew Lexicon entry for Tsel," s.v. "shadow," Genesis 19:8. Available from <http://www.biblestudytools.net/Lexicons/Hebrew/heb.cgi?number=673 8&version=kjv>.

[3] Brown, Driver, Briggs and Gesenius, "Hebrew Lexicon entry for D@muwth," s.v. "likeness," Genesis 1:26. Available from <http://www.biblestudytools.net/Lexicons/Hebrew/heb.cgi?number=182 3&version=kjv>.

[4] Ibid., "Hebrew Lexicon entry for 'elohiym,' s.v. "God," Genesis 1. Available from <http://www.biblestudytools.net/Lexicons/Hebrew/ heb.cgi?number=430&version=kjv>.

[5] Ibid., "Hebrew Lexicon entry for Y@hovah," s.v. "Lord," Genesis 2:7. Available from <http://www.biblestudytools.net/Lexicons/Hebrew/ heb.cgi?number=3068&version=kjv>.

[6] Based on a definition from Brown, Driver, Briggs and Gesenius, "Hebrew Lexicon entry for Yatsar," s.v. "form," Genesis 2:7. Available from <http://www.biblestudytools.net/Lexicons/Hebrew/heb.cgi?number=333 5&version=kjv>.

[7] Ibid, "Hebrew Lexicon entry for Nephesh," s.v. "soul," Genesis 2:7. Available from <http://www.biblestudytools.net/Lexicons/Hebrew/ heb.cgi?number=5315&version=kjv>.

[8] Ibid., "Hebrew Lexicon entry for Ruwach," s.v. "breath," Genesis 1:2; 6:17. Available from <http://www.biblestudytools.net/Lexicons/Hebrew/ heb.cgi?number=7307&version=kjv>.

⁹ Ibid., "Hebrew Lexicon entry for Nephesh, s.v. "soul," Genesis <http://www.biblestudytools.net/Lexicons/Hebrew/heb.cgi?number=531 5&version=kjv>.

¹⁰ Thayer and Smith, *The KJV New Testament Greek Lexicon,* "Greek Lexicon entry for *Rhema*," s.v. "word," Romans 10:17. Available from <http://www.biblestudytools.net/Lexicons/Greek/grk.cgi?number=4487& version=kjv>.

¹¹ Based on a definition from Thayer and Smith, "Greek Lexicon entry for Eis," s.v. "unto," Romans 10:10. Available from <http://www.biblestudytools.net/Lexicons/Greek/grk.cgi?number=1519&version=kjv>.

¹² Based on a definition from Thayer and Smith, "Greek Lexicon entry for Sozo," s.v. "save," Matthew 1:21. Available from <http://www.bible studytools.net/Lexicons/Greek/grk.cgi?number=4982&version=kjv>.

¹³ Ibid., "Greek Lexicon entry for Homologeo," s.v. "confess," Matthew 10:32. Available from <http://www.biblestudytools.net/Lexicons/ Greek/grk.cgi?number=3670&version=kjv>.

¹⁴ Based on a definition in Thayer and Smith, "Greek Lexicon entry for Stoma," s.v. "mouth," Romans 10:8-10. Available from <http://www.bible studytools.net/Lexicons/Greek/grk.cgi?number=4750&version=kjv>.

Chapter 9

¹ Thayer and Smith, "Greek Lexicon entry for Bema," s.v. "seat," Romans 14:10. Available from <http://www.biblestudytools.net/Lexicons/Greek/ grk.cgi?number=968&version=kjv>.

Chapter 10

¹ Based on a definition from Thayer and Smith, "Greek Lexicon entry for Kauchaomai," s.v. "rejoice," Romans 5:2. Available from <http://www.biblestudytools.net/Lexicons/Greek/grk.cgi?number=2744& version=kjv>.

Scriptures—More Verses on Hope

¹ Thayer and Smith, "Greek Lexicon entry for Elpis," s.v. "hope." Available from <http://www.biblestudytools.net/Lexicons/Greek/grk.cgi?number= 1680&version=kjv>.

² Ibid.

Prayer of Salvation

God loves you—no matter who you are, no matter what your past. God loves you so much that He gave His one and only begotten Son for you. The Bible tells us that "...whoever believes in him shall not perish but have eternal life" (John 3:16 NIV). Jesus laid down His life and rose again so that we could spend eternity with Him in heaven and experience His absolute best on earth. If you would like to receive Jesus into your life, say the following prayer out loud and mean it from your heart.

Heavenly Father, I come to You admitting that I am a sinner. Right now, I choose to turn away from sin, and I ask You to cleanse me of all unrighteousness. I believe that Your Son, Jesus, died on the cross to take away my sins. I also believe that He rose again from the dead so that I might be forgiven of my sins and made right - eous through faith in Him. I call upon the name of Jesus Christ to be the Savior and Lord of my life. Jesus, I choose to follow You and ask that You fill me with the power of the Holy Spirit. I declare that right now I am a child of God. I am free from sin and full of the righteousness of God. I am saved in Jesus' name. Amen.

If you prayed this prayer to receive Jesus Christ as your Savior for the first time, please contact us on the Web at **www.harrisonhouse.com** to receive a free book.

Or you may write to us at

Harrison House
P.O. Box 35035
Tulsa, Oklahoma 74153

About the Author

Terry Law, the president and founder of World Compassion/Terry Law Ministries, was born in Meadow Lake, Saskatchewan, a backwater town on the Canadian prairie. His father, a rural preacher, hunted to provide food for his family.

At an early age, Terry was aware that God was calling him to an international preaching ministry. He fought that call during his teen years and planned instead to study law to become involved in Canadian politics. Through a dramatic conversion, Terry was brought up short by the Lord, and he found himself a few days later in Bible school, preparing for full-time ministry.

Terry, along with his college friend Larry Dalton, founded Living Sound, a contemporary Christian Music Group in 1969. They began to travel across the United States and Canada in preparation for their first overseas ministry trip to Africa in 1970. It was during that mission trip that God spoke to Terry in an audible way, "I am going to send you to minister to the closed nations of the world. You will do things there that most men would believe impossible. If you trust Me and are obedient, I will protect you." From that day to this, Terry and his team have walked by those marching orders.

Terry has been ministering the Gospel in dangerous places for 35 years and has preached in over 60 nations, including countries like Russia and the Republics of the former Soviet Union, China, India, Vietnam, Laos, Burma, Nepal, Pakistan, Afghanistan, and most recently Iraq. Terry Law is one of America's foremost speakers on praise and worship and is in demand as a missionary statesman throughout the world.

In 1990, while passing out Bibles in Russia, Terry heard a woman declare, "We can't eat your Bibles!" This resonated deeply in Terry, and that same year "World Compassion" was formed to help meet the needs of people who were not only in need of the Gospel, but also in need of food and medicine. World Compassion/Terry Law Ministries has moved to meet these needs, and many lives have been changed as a result. Over 600 tons of food have been distributed since World Compassion began.

Since September 11, 2001, World Compassion Terry Law Ministries has focused on Afghanistan and Iraq. Through the delivery of humanitarian aid, God has opened doors for Terry to go into refugee camps to light a candle of hope through the ministering of the Gospel in the darkness of postwar Afghanistan. A church plant in Afghanistan is already ministering to more than 500 people.

Terry and his organization, World Compassion, have teamed with International Health Services Foundation to provide a medical clinic for Kabul University, through which medical care, along with prayer, is offered to the students and faculty of the premier school in the country. World Compassion is also building homes for widows in Kabul, as well as helping to provide training for widows and their families in sewing, print-making, gardening, and English language acquisition.

Doors have also opened in Iraq through humanitarian aid and Christian literature; many lives are being changed in this new harvest field. God has enabled Terry to establish connections at the highest levels of government in these countries and in our own country, as well. Plans are being laid for the planting of two Signs and Wonders churches in northern and central Iraq.

In addition, Terry is the author of several best-selling books, including: *The Power of Praise and Worship; Praise Releases Faith; How to Enter the Presence of God;* and his most recent book, *The Truth About Angels.*

Terry resides in Tulsa, Oklahoma.

Other Books Available From Terry Law Ministries:

The Power of Praise and Worship

Praise Releases Faith

How to Enter the Presence of God

The Truth about Angels

To contact Terry Law please write to:

World Compassion
Terry Law Ministries
P.O. Box 92
Tulsa, Oklahoma 74101
Phone: 918.492.2858
Fax: 918.496.9073

Or visit him on the Web at:
www.worldcompassion.tv

Please include your prayer requests and comments when you write.

www.harrisonhouse.com

Fast. Easy. Convenient!

- ◆ New Book Information
- ◆ Look Inside the Book
- ◆ Press Releases
- ◆ Bestsellers
- ◆ Free E-News
- ◆ Author Biographies

- ◆ Upcoming Books
- ◆ Share Your Testimony
- ◆ Online Product Availability
- ◆ Product Specials
- ◆ Order Online

For the latest in book news and author information, please visit us on the Web at www.harrisonhouse.com. Get up-to-date pictures and details on all our powerful and life-changing products. Sign up for our e-mail newsletter, *Friends of the House,* and receive free monthly information on our authors and products including testimonials, author announcements, and more!

Harrison House—
Books That Bring Hope, Books That Bring Change

The Harrison House Vision

Proclaiming the truth and the power
Of the Gospel of Jesus Christ
With excellence;

Challenging Christians to
Live victoriously,
Grow spiritually,
Know God intimately.